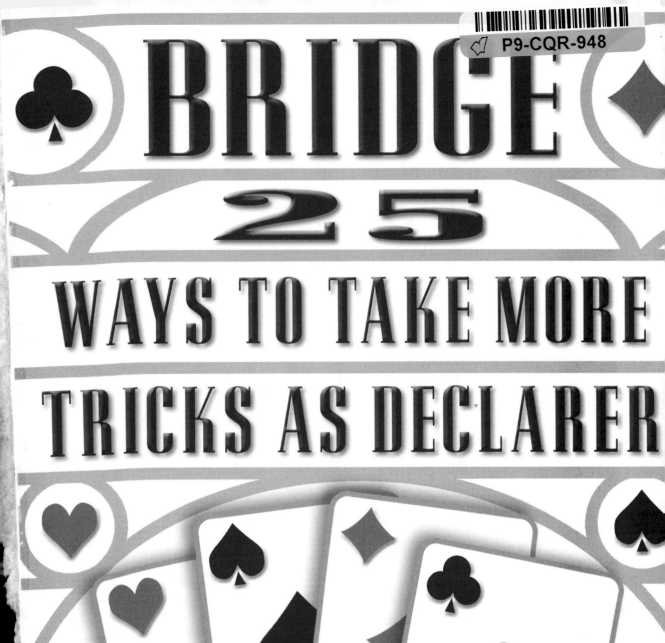

BRIDGE
25
WAYS TO TAKE MORE
TRICKS AS DECLARER

MASTER POINT PRESS • TORONTO

Master Point Press
331 Douglas Ave.
Toronto, Ontario Canada
M5M 1H2
(416) 781-0351 Fax (416) 781-1831
Internet www.masterpointpress.com

Canadian Cataloguing in Publication Data
Seagram, Barbara
Bridge: 25 Ways to take more tricks as declarer/ Barbara Seagram & David Bird.

ISBN 1-894154-47-9
ISBN 978-1-894154-47-5

1. Contract bridge — Bidding. I. Bird, David, 1946 — II. Title.
GV1282.4.S419 2003   795.41'52   C2001-904151-9

Editor	Ray Lee
Cover and interior design	Olena S. Sullivan/New Mediatrix
Interior format and copyediting	Deanna Bourassa

Printed and bound in Canada by Webcom

8 7 6 5 4   08 09 10 11 12

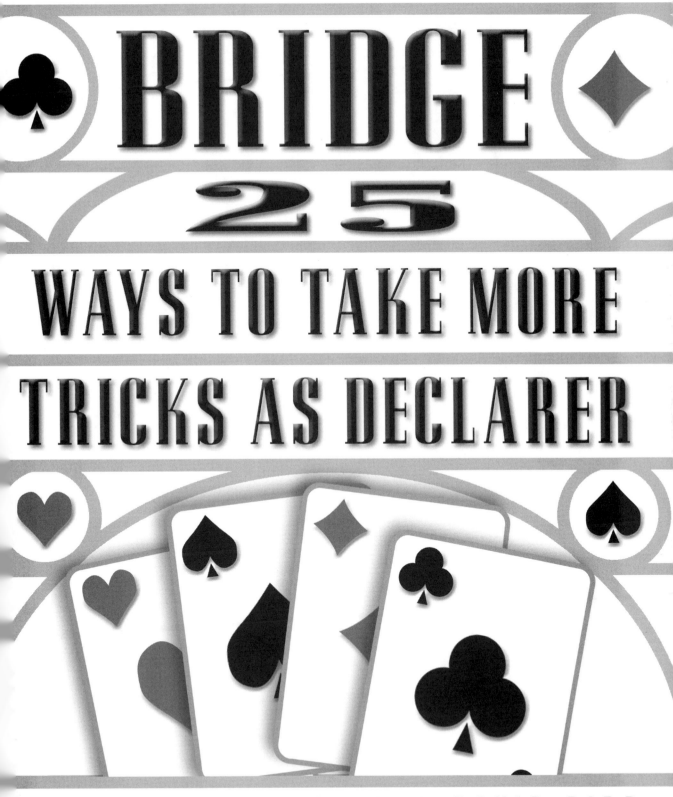

BRIDGE
25
WAYS TO TAKE MORE
TRICKS AS DECLARER

BARBARA SEAGRAM & DAVID BIRD

To my children, Heather & Christopher. How did I ever get so lucky?

Barbara Seagram

For my two children — Claire and James. I'm proud of you both!

David Bird

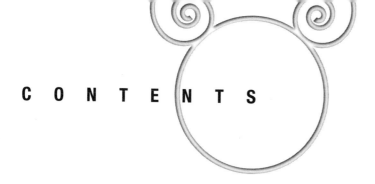

CONTENTS

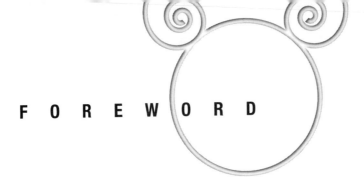

F O R E W O R D

I predict that this book will become one of the most well-used books you own. Barbara Seagram and David Bird have clearly formed one of those things that all bridge players strive to achieve — a successful partnership — and they demonstrate the effectiveness of that partnership in this book. David has provided the bridge expertise and insightfulness of a true expert while Barbara displays a knack for teaching the game that few possess.

From the very first chapter, they tackle subject matter that seems to confuse many beginning and intermediate bridge players. And they do it in a way that is easily comprehensible. At each point of every chapter readers are taken through the steps they should be considering as they tackle the various problems. Additionally, the lessons are layered so that readers become more adept at identifying just what type of problem they are facing on a given hand. It is clear to me that most advanced players don't remember what a struggle it was to learn the material covered in this book. And how once it had been learned, they needed constant review to solidify that knowledge.

During a recent mentoring program, a student told my wife: 'I know I'm supposed to be thinking — I just don't know what I'm supposed to be thinking about!' Digesting this book will solve one of the major problems faced by these students; I know that these are topics that have frequently left my own students befuddled and convinced that they will never get them. I am looking forward to using this material as a textbook in my own classes. It has been so long since teachers have had such a textbook available!

This book is must reading for you and your favorite partner. But you are going to need two copies between you, because you won't want to be without your own!

Alan LeBendig,
December 2002

I N T R O D U C T I O N

For some readers, we realize, this may be your very first bridge book.

First, may we congratulate you. What a great choice you made! Secondly, we need to point out a few things that all bridge books and bridge columns have in common. The declarer always sits South, with the opening lead made by West. The hand diagrams will therefore match your experience at the bridge table when you are declarer. The dummy is ahead of you and the opening lead is made by the player to your left.

Bridge is more technical than a game such as Blackjack and has its own terminology. There is no need for you to be worried about this. We will explain all technical terms, the first time they are used. If you come across any term that you do not understand you can look it up in the Glossary at the end of the book.

Finally, perhaps you are not sure that bridge is the right pastime for you and are wondering if you should have bought that book on open-water kayaking instead. Have no such doubts. Bridge is the finest game in the world, with a vast army of players who will become your immediate friends the moment you meet them.

Right, it's time to turn the page and get reading!

Barbara Seagram and David Bird

C H A P T E R

THE SIMPLE FINESSE

 A very common lead with inexperienced players is the lead of a queen in a suit from hand up to a guarded ace in the other hand, not holding the knave or ten in either hand. What can be gained by it? **W. Dalton.** *Practical Bridge. 1908*

One of the most important techniques in cardplay is also one of the simplest — you lead towards a high card that you are hoping to make. Look at this familiar layout:

```
                  ♠ K 8
                 ┌─────┐
                 │  N  │
♠ A J 9 4 2      │W   E│      ♠ Q 10 6 5
                 │  S  │
                 └─────┘
                  ♠ 7 3
```

To score a trick with the king you must lead from the South hand, towards dummy's king. If West plays his ace, the king will become good. If instead he plays low, you will rise with dummy's king and it will win the trick. You have a 50% chance of success. You will score a trick when West holds the ace but not when East has it.

If you mistakenly lead the suit from dummy, you will have practically no chance of making the king. The defenders will win the first round cheaply and the ace will capture dummy's king on the second round.

Sometimes you have to lead twice towards the honors in a suit:

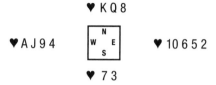

Hoping to score both the king and the queen, you lead towards the dummy. If West rises with the ace, the king and queen become good. If he plays low, the king will win and you will return to the South hand in some different suit to lead towards the queen. It makes no difference when West decides to take the ace — you will score two tricks. Once again this has a 50% chance of success. If East held the ♥A, you would make only one trick.

Look back at the diagram. What would happen if you made the mistake of leading the king from dummy instead? West would win with the ace and you would score only one heart trick.

There is no reason why the lead towards a high card should be on the first round of the suit. Look at these two combinations:

In position (1) you play the ace on the first round and then lead towards the queen, the honor that you hope will give you a second trick. The queen will score when East holds the king. In position (2) you cash the ace and king and then lead towards the jack on the third round. You will score a third trick in three cases: when the queen falls on the first two rounds, when West holds the queen and when the suit breaks 3-3 (making your last diamond a winner).

Sometimes the honor that you lead towards is accompanied by a higher non-touching honor. This is the most familiar form of the play known as a **finesse**:

3)	♥ A Q 3	4)	♦ K J 8
	♥ 8 4		♦ A 6 3

In (3) you lead low to the queen, hoping that West holds the king. In (4) you play the ace on the first round and then lead low to the jack. You hope that West holds the queen.

Even when you hold only the queen you can sometimes set up a trick:

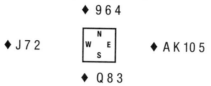

♦ 9 6 4

♦ J 7 2   ♦ A K 10 5

♦ Q 8 3

You lead low from dummy and East has to rise with the ace or king to prevent you from scoring an immediate trick with the queen. When you regain the lead, you cross to dummy in a different suit and lead again towards the queen. East has to rise with his remaining top honor and your queen is now good. You were lucky to find East with both top honors, yes, but if you had led the suit from the South hand you would have wasted this piece of good fortune.

Let's see a whole deal where you can make the contract by leading towards high cards.

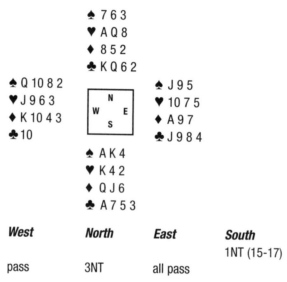

♠ 7 6 3
♥ A Q 8
♦ 8 5 2
♣ K Q 6 2

♠ Q 10 8 2
♥ J 9 6 3
♦ K 10 4 3
♣ 10

♠ J 9 5
♥ 10 7 5
♦ A 9 7
♣ J 9 8 4

♠ A K 4
♥ K 4 2
♦ Q J 6
♣ A 7 5 3

West	North	East	South
			1NT (15-17)
pass	3NT	all pass	

West leads a fourth-best ♠2 against your contract of 3NT. You can count eight top tricks (two spades, three hearts and three clubs). If clubs break 3-2 you will have a fourth trick in that suit, which will give you the contract.

You win the spade lead and test the club suit by playing the ace and king. Bad news comes when West shows out on the second round. You have only eight tricks now. Where can you find a ninth? You must hope to make a diamond trick by leading twice towards the queen and jack. You will succeed unless West holds both the ace and king. At Trick 4 you lead a diamond from dummy. East plays low and your queen loses to West's king. You win the next spade trick and cross to dummy with the ♥A, to lead a second round of diamonds. East plays low and you rise with the jack. This time you are in luck. East holds the missing ace and your jack wins the trick. You now have nine tricks.

Note how important it was to lead **towards** those diamond honors. What would have happened if you had led the queen from your hand on the first round? East would have won with the ace and, with West's K-10 sitting over your J-6, you would fail to score a diamond trick. Down one!

Finessing by leading a high card

Until now, we have led a low card towards the combination that we wanted to finesse. Sometimes you lead a high card:

♦ A 6 3

♦ K 9 7 2   ♦ 8 5 4

♦ Q J 10

You lead the diamond queen, playing low from dummy unless the king appears. If the queen wins the first round, West playing low, you will lead the jack next. Any time that West chooses to play his king, the guillotine will fall — you will win with dummy's ace.

This position is similar:

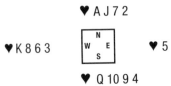

♥ A J 7 2

♥ K 8 6 3   ♥ 5

♥ Q 10 9 4

If you start with a low card to the jack, you will be in the wrong hand to repeat the finesse. (You would have to return to your hand in a different suit.) It is more convenient to lead the ♥Q on the first round.

In the previous two positions you do not mind in the slightest if the honor you lead is covered by the defender in second seat. Why is that? Because you hold sufficient neighboring cards to take the remaining tricks if the opponents cover. The next combination does not pass this test:

♣ A Q 7 4

♣ K 8   ♣ 10 9 3

♣ J 6 5 2

Your only chance of four tricks is to find West with a doubleton king. You should play low to the queen on the first round and then cash the ace. If you mistakenly lead the jack on the first round, you will squander your good fortune. West will cover when he holds a doubleton king and East will score an undeserved trick.

This position is similar:

♠ A J 7 5 3

♠ K   ♠ 10 9 2

♠ Q 8 6 4

You cannot afford to lead the queen. It will be covered by the king and ace and once again East will score an undeserved trick. Lead a low card instead, intending to finesse dummy's jack, and all will be well. Dummy's ace will capture the stiff king on the first round and you will score all five tricks.

Many players go wrong on this simple-looking combination:

BY THE WAY

The term 'stiff king' means a king that is unaccompanied by any smaller cards. It is alternatively known as a 'singleton king' or a 'bare king'.

♠ A 7 3

♠ Q J 5 2

How would you give yourself the best chance of three tricks?

You often see players leading the queen from the South hand, but there is little point in it. If East wins with the king, you will need a 3-3 break to make three tricks (only a 36% chance). If instead West holds the king, he will cover at some stage and again you will need a 3-3 break.

A much better idea is to cash the ace and lead twice towards the queen-jack. You then make three tricks not only when the suit breaks 3-3 but also when East holds the king (or West has a singleton king). By playing the suit correctly, you increase your chance from 36% to a massive 68%.

Give yourself one more neighboring card, making the South holding Q-J-10-5, and the situation would change. With three tricks now assured, you could afford to lead the queen and play low from dummy if West did not produce the king. You would then score all four tricks when West held K-x-x.

The two-way finesse

Sometimes you have what is known as a 'two-way finesse':

♠ A 10 5

♠ K J 6

If you think that West has the missing queen, you will finesse dummy's ten. If instead you think that East holds the queen, you will finesse the jack. Unless there is a specific clue from the bidding, you should play the other suits first, trying to discover which defender holds the majority of the missing spades. You will then finesse that player for the queen.

This position is similar:

♥ K 9 3

♥ Q 10 4

You are bound to lose one trick to the ace but you can finesse either defender for the missing jack. Again you would play on the other suits and place the missing jack in the hand of the defender who appeared to hold more hearts.

Should I finesse or play for the drop?

When you are missing the queen, there is an easy-to-remember rule that tells you whether to finesse or play for the drop: *Eight ever, nine never.* What does that mean? It means you should finesse when you hold eight cards between the hands but not when you hold nine cards.

♥ K J 6 3

♥ A 7 5 4

Here you hold eight cards. You should cash the ace first, in case East holds a singleton queen, and then play low to the jack. *Eight ever.* A finesse is a 50-50 proposition but the queen will fall in two rounds only 33% of the time if you play the ace and king instead.

♣ A J 8 6 3

♣ K 7 4 2

You now have nine cards between the two hands and should play the king first. Unless East shows out, you then play low to the ace. *Nine never.*

The odds are strongly in favor of a finesse with a combined holding of eight cards. With nine cards, the odds are only marginally in favor of playing for the drop. Suppose, in the last position, that your right-hand opponent has already shown up with a long suit elsewhere. He is likely to be shorter than his partner in clubs, so you would finesse West for the ♣Q.

When you are missing the king, you should finesse when you hold ten or fewer cards between the hands and play for the drop with eleven cards.

♠ A J 9 8 4 2

♠ Q 10 7 6

With a combined holding of ten cards you lead the queen and run it if West plays low. (The argument 'West would have covered if he held the king, so I might as well hope for a singleton king with East' applies only against very weak defenders. A good player would not dream of covering from K-x or K-x-x if you have bid that suit.) Give yourself a fifth spade in the South hand, making it eleven spades between the two hands, and you should play for the drop.

Should I cash a high card before finessing?

With some combinations you should try to drop a possible singleton honor before taking a finesse in the suit:

♥ A K 9 2

♥ J 10 5 3

You have a combined holding of eight cards, so the odds favor a finesse against the queen rather than playing for the drop. However, by playing dummy's ace before taking a finesse, you avoid losing to a singleton queen with East.

What do you make of this combination, which looks similar?

♦ A K J 10 9 3

♦ 6 4

Again you have eight cards and intend to finesse West for the queen. Should you cash the ace first, in case East holds a singleton queen?

You should not cash the ace first. You would pick up a singleton queen with East, yes, but you would lose out when East held a singleton eight, seven, five or two. (Only one subsequent finesse would be possible and you would not be able to pick up West's Q-x-x-x.) This is a reminder that you have to think at this game, not merely apply a set of rules!

Summary

✓ By leading towards any honor that is not a winner, you increase the chance of scoring a trick with it. Lead towards a king, for example, and you score a trick whenever the king sits over the defender's ace.

✓ When you hold a combination of honors, for example K-Q-x or A-Q-J-x, you may need to lead towards them twice.

THE SIMPLE FINESSE

NOW TRY THESE...

1)

♠ 7 6 5 2
♥ 10 6 3
♦ 8 5 2
♣ K 8 6

```
      N
  W       E
      S
```

♠ A K
♥ A K Q J 4
♦ K Q 7
♣ A Q 5

West leads the ♠Q against 6NT. How will you play the slam?

2)

♠ A Q 7 2
♥ Q 5 3
♦ 10 8 6 3
♣ 7 5

```
      N
  W       E
      S
```

♠ K J 9
♥ A 8 7 2
♦ A 7 5 4
♣ A K

West leads the ♣Q against 3NT. How will you play the hand?

3)

♠ A
♥ 8 6 4 3
♦ 8 7 4 2
♣ A 7 6 3

```
      N
  W       E
      S
```

♠ K 7 6 3
♥ A K
♦ Q J 5
♣ K Q J 8

West leads the ♠2 against 3NT. How will you play the hand?

ANSWERS

1) You have ten top tricks (in other words, tricks ready to take) outside diamonds. To bring your total to twelve tricks you will need to lead twice towards your king-queen of diamonds, hoping that East holds the ace. Fortunately you do have two entries to dummy — the ♣K and the ♥10. You win the spade lead, cross to the ♥10 and play a diamond to the king. When this wins the trick, you return to dummy with the ♣K. There is nothing East can do when you lead another diamond towards your hand. Whether or not he rises with the ace, you will score a trick with your queen of diamonds, bringing your total to twelve. (When West holds the ♦A you will go down. There is nothing you can do about it.)

2) You can count eight top tricks. The best chance of a ninth is to lead towards dummy's ♥Q. If West holds the king, the queen will score a trick, bringing your total to nine. Playing diamonds instead is no good. Even if the suit divides 3-2, the defenders are almost certain to score two diamonds and at least three clubs before you can bring your own total to nine.

3) You can count eight top tricks. Since the lead strongly suggests that spades are 4-4, the best chance for a ninth trick is to lead towards the diamond honors twice. Unless West holds both the ace and king, you will be able to establish a ninth trick from the suit. Win the spade lead and play a diamond to the queen. Win the spade return, cross to dummy with the ace of clubs and lead a diamond to the jack. If East holds either or both of the top diamond honors, you will make the contract.

RUFFING LOSERS

 When declarer does not lead trumps, he probably wants to make some little trumps by ruffing.
W. Dalton. *Practical Bridge. 1908*

Playing in a suit contract, rather than in notrump, gives you two big advantages. You can ruff to stop the defenders from scoring tricks in their own best suit. You can also score extra tricks by ruffing losers in the dummy.

Let's start by looking at a straightforward deal where you need to score ruffs in the dummy.

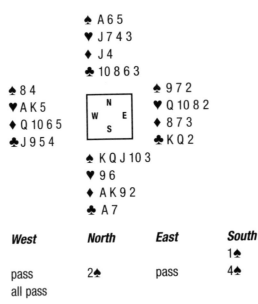

	♠ A 6 5		
	♥ J 7 4 3		
	♦ J 4		
	♣ 10 8 6 3		

♠ 8 4		♠ 9 7 2
♥ A K 5	N	♥ Q 10 8 2
♦ Q 10 6 5	W E	♦ 8 7 3
♣ J 9 5 4	S	♣ K Q 2

	♠ K Q J 10 3	
	♥ 9 6	
	♦ A K 9 2	
	♣ A 7	

West	North	East	South
			1♠
pass	2♠	pass	4♠
all pass			

West leads the ace of hearts and continues with king and another heart. You ruff the third round and see that you have an unavoidable third loser in clubs. To restrict your losers to three, you must therefore ruff both of your losing diamonds.

BY THE WAY

A 'loser' is a potential losing trick. With ♦A-7-3 opposite ♦9-6-2 you would have two diamond 'losers'. The ace would win the first diamond trick but the opponents would then win the next two diamond tricks.

Suppose you make the mistake of drawing trumps straight away by playing three rounds of spades. Not a promising start, is it? With no trumps left in dummy you would not be able to ruff any diamonds. Instead, at Trick 4, after ruffing the third round of hearts, you should play the ace and king of diamonds. You then lead a third round of diamonds and ruff in dummy with a low trump. A club to the ace returns the lead to your hand and you ruff your last diamond with the trump ace. East has no more diamonds but he cannot overruff because you saved dummy's ace of trumps for the fourth round of diamonds. The time has come to draw trumps! You will concede a club trick at the end and make your contract exactly.

How many trump tricks did you score on that last contract? Five in your hand, by drawing trumps, and two more by taking ruffs in the dummy. That's a total of seven. Each time you take a ruff in the hand with fewer trumps (usually called the 'short-trump hand'), you score an extra trick.

Ruffing in the 'long-trump hand' brings no such reward. Suppose you had surrendered an early club trick and taken a club ruff or two in the South hand. This would be quite useless. You would make just five trump tricks — the same number you could have made by drawing trumps. That's because the trumps in the (long-trump) South hand are winners anyway.

Sometimes you have to do some work to prepare for a ruff.

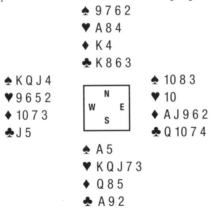

West leads the ♠K against your game in hearts. Three certain losers stare you in the face — a spade, a club and the ace of diamonds. To avoid losing a second diamond trick, you must take a diamond ruff in the dummy. Once again it would make no sense to draw trumps immediately. After winning the spade lead, you should instead play a diamond to the king, preparing the way for a diamond ruff. East wins with the ace, cashes the ♠10 and plays another spade. You ruff low and play the queen of diamonds. You then ruff your remaining diamond. Should you ruff with the ace or with a low trump? What do you think?

If you ruff with the ace, you will lose a trump trick when either defender started with four trumps. It is better to ruff with the eight, taking the much smaller risk of East holding only two diamonds and being able to overruff. You can then draw trumps, in four rounds if necessary, and score ten tricks for the contract.

Let's look at a deal where you do need to ruff high.

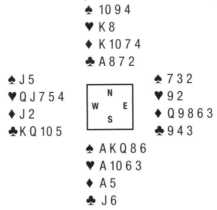

West leads the ♣K against your adventurous small slam in spades. You win with the ace and note that you have a certain loser in clubs. The only way to dispose of your two heart losers is to ruff them. You play the king and ace of hearts and lead a third round. Suppose you ruff with dummy's ♠4. East will overruff with the seven and you will go down.

Never send a boy to do a man's job! Instead of ruffing the third round of hearts with the four, you should ruff with the ten. This reduces the chance that you will be overruffed. East has only two hearts but is unable to overruff the ten. You play a diamond to the ace and ruff your last heart with the nine. The only task remaining is to draw trumps. As you see, ruffing high can work well, even when you are not ruffing with a master trump.

Suppose there are only two trumps in dummy, one high and the other not, and you need to take two ruffs. You will need to think carefully about whether you should take the first ruff with the high trump. Look at this deal:

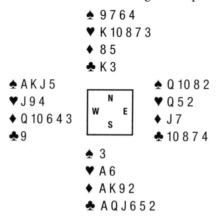

```
                    ♠ 9 7 6 4
                    ♥ K 10 8 7 3
                    ♦ 8 5
                    ♣ K 3
  ♠ A K J 5                          ♠ Q 10 8 2
  ♥ J 9 4              N             ♥ Q 5 2
  ♦ Q 10 6 4 3     W       E         ♦ J 7
  ♣ 9                  S             ♣ 10 8 7 4
                    ♠ 3
                    ♥ A 6
                    ♦ A K 9 2
                    ♣ A Q J 6 5 2
```

Suppose you are in a contract of five clubs and West leads the two top spades. You ruff the second round and see that you must reduce your two diamond losers to one. Since there are only two diamonds in dummy, and West did not switch to a trump, you have a chance to ruff both your diamond losers.

Suppose you play the ace and king of diamonds and ruff the third round of diamonds with the three of trumps. East will overruff and return a trump, removing dummy's last trump. You cannot avoid a subsequent diamond loser and will go down.

BY THE WAY

It makes no difference if East declines to overruff the fourth round of diamonds. You will still lose just one spade and one trump trick.

To give yourself the best chance of making the club game, you should ruff the third round of diamonds with the king. East shows out but he cannot overruff. You then return to the South hand with the ace of hearts and ruff your last diamond with the three of trumps. Why do you do this, when you know that East will be able to overruff? Just in case East holds four trumps. His overruff will then be the second and last trick for the defense. Had you tried to draw trumps instead, your A-Q-J could not have picked up East's 10-8-7-4. You would have lost a spade trick, a diamond trick and a trump trick. Down one!

Before we leave this deal behind, how would you have played it in the higher contract of six clubs? The only chance would be to ruff the third round of diamonds with a low trump, return to the South hand with the heart ace and ruff your last diamond with the king. You would then return to your hand with a spade ruff and try to draw trumps with the A-Q-J. All would be well if diamonds broke 4-3 and the trumps broke 3-2.

You can sometimes avoid an overruff by drawing some of the enemy trumps but not all.

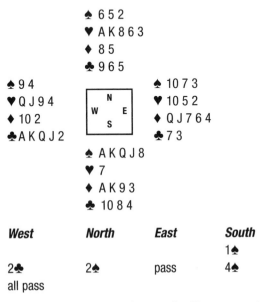

	♠ 6 5 2	
	♥ A K 8 6 3	
	♦ 8 5	
	♣ 9 6 5	
♠ 9 4		♠ 10 7 3
♥ Q J 9 4		♥ 10 5 2
♦ 10 2		♦ Q J 7 6 4
♣ A K Q J 2		♣ 7 3
	♠ A K Q J 8	
	♥ 7	
	♦ A K 9 3	
	♣ 10 8 4	

West	North	East	South
			1♠
2♣	2♠	pass	4♠
all pass			

West cashes three clubs and switches to the ♥Q, won with the ace. You can throw one of your diamond losers on the heart king. The other diamond loser will have to be ruffed. Suppose you play ace, king and another diamond immediately. West will say 'Thank you very much' and ruff with the nine, beating the contract. Instead you should draw two rounds of trumps before attempting the ruff. As the cards lie, West will then be out of trumps when you lead the third round of diamonds. You will ruff with dummy's last trump, the six, and make the game.

Occasionally you can prepare for a ruff by creating a shortage in dummy. You do this by discarding a loser from dummy on a winner in your hand. Here is a full-deal example:

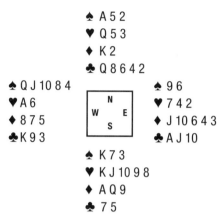

♠ A 5 2
♥ Q 5 3
♦ K 2
♣ Q 8 6 4 2

♠ Q J 10 8 4
♥ A 6
♦ 8 7 5
♣ K 9 3

♠ 9 6
♥ 7 4 2
♦ J 10 6 4 3
♣ A J 10

♠ K 7 3
♥ K J 10 9 8
♦ A Q 9
♣ 7 5

West leads the ♠Q against your heart game and you count the possible losers in the South hand. There are two club losers and one trump loser. How can you avoid a further loser in the spade suit?

You will not have time to set up the club suit before the defenders develop a spade winner. How about playing three rounds of diamonds, throwing a spade from dummy? That looks promising. With only two spades left in dummy, you will be able to take a spade ruff.

How does the play go? You win the spade lead with the ace and play the king, ace and queen of diamonds, throwing a spade from dummy. The ♠K is followed by a third round of spades, ruffed with dummy's queen. (If you ruff with a low trump instead, East will defeat the game by overruffing.) You have scored six tricks already and the K-J-10-9-8 of trumps will generate four more tricks to bring the total to ten.

Summary

- ✓ When you have losers in your hand facing two cards or fewer in the dummy, you can often ruff the losers. (For example, with ♦A-K-7-3 opposite ♦9-5 you will aim to ruff two diamond losers.)

- ✓ Usually, aim to take ruffs in the dummy (the short-trump hand) rather than in your hand.

- ✓ Do not draw trumps immediately if this will prevent you from taking the planned ruffs.

- ✓ Ruff with a high trump whenever you can afford to do so. This avoids the risk of an overruff.

RUFFING LOSERS

NOW TRY THESE...

1)

♠ A J 3
♥ A 8 6 3
♦ A 2
♣ K 9 6 2

```
      N
   W     E
      S
```

♠ K Q 10 9 4
♥ K Q 4
♦ J 8 3
♣ A 5

West leads a low trump against 6♠. How will you play the contract?

2)

♠ 8 7 3
♥ K 5 3
♦ 7 6 5 2
♣ K 8 3

```
      N
   W     E
      S
```

♠ A K 6 2
♥ A 10
♦ A K
♣ A Q J 10 5

West leads the ♦J against 6♣. How will you play the contract?

3)

♠ A 5 3
♥ A 2
♦ 8 6 4
♣ 10 8 5 3 2

```
      N
   W     E
      S
```

♠ K Q J 10 7 2
♥ K Q 4
♦ A K J
♣ 4

West leads the ace and king of clubs against 6♠. How will you play?

ANSWERS

1) Your only losers are in diamonds, where you have two potential losing cards. How can you eliminate one of these losers? One possibility is that the heart suit will break 3-3, allowing you to discard a diamond loser. That relies on luck, though, and a better idea is to ruff a diamond in dummy. After winning the trump lead, you should play ace and another diamond. Win the return in your hand and ruff a diamond with the ace or jack of trumps. (Ruffing high avoids the risk of an overruff.) You can then draw trumps.

   Note that you cannot afford to draw even one more round of trumps before ducking a diamond. If you do, the defenders may remove dummy's last trump when they gain the lead. You will not then be able to take a diamond ruff.

2) This time you have two potential losers in spades. Suppose you draw trumps and play ace, king and another spade. You will make the contract when spades break 3-3. Are you happy with that? No, because a 3-3 break is only a 36% chance. Most of the time you would go down. Once again, a better idea is to take a ruff — to ruff the fourth round of spades in dummy. After winning the diamond lead you should play king, ace and another spade immediately. Unless the suit happens to break 3-3, you will ruff your fourth spade when you regain the lead. Since your trumps are very strong, you can afford to ruff with the king to prevent an overruff.

3) The spades and hearts are solid. To make the slam you will have to avoid a diamond loser. Hands up those of you who are intending to take a diamond finesse! It's not the best idea because, once again, you would be relying on luck. A simple finesse works only 50% of the time. A better idea is to play three rounds of hearts, discarding a diamond from dummy. Once you have created a diamond shortage in dummy, you will be able to ruff the jack of diamonds.

   After ruffing the second round of clubs, you should draw two rounds of trumps with the king and queen. If trumps break 2-2, you will be able to take your diamond ruff in complete safety. Let's assume they break 3-1. Leaving the ace of trumps in dummy, you play three rounds of hearts, throwing a diamond from dummy. You then play the ace and king of diamonds and ruff the ♦J with dummy's ace of trumps. You return to your hand by ruffing a club high and can then draw the last trump, proceeding to make the rest of the tricks.

C H A P T E R **3**

ESTABLISHING A SUIT

 As soon as the dummy is exposed, you can see at a glance what suit can readily be established between the two hands, and the small cards of it made as useful as aces and kings.
W. Dalton. *Practical Bridge. 1908*

Suppose you are the declarer, sitting South, and this is the diamond layout:

♦ A K 8 6 5 2

♦ Q 10 4   ♦ J 3

♦ 9 7

The diamond suit is not ready to run, so you will have to **establish** it. What does that mean? You must remove West's stopper in the suit, so you can score tricks with the long cards.

If the contract is in notrump, you might play the ace and king and then surrender a third round to West's queen. The remaining three cards in dummy would then be good. Alternatively you might duck the first round of diamonds, playing low cards from both hands. This would often be better, since you would still have an entry in the diamond suit itself to reach the established winners.

Playing in a suit contract, you could establish the suit without giving up a diamond trick. You would play the ace and king, as before, and then ruff the third round. Once again, the three low cards in dummy would become good.

Let's see a whole deal where you need to establish a long suit in the dummy.

```
                    ♠ J 7 2
                    ♥ K 5 2
                    ♦ J 4
                    ♣ A K 9 8 6
       ♠ A K Q 6 4        N        ♠ 8 5
       ♥ 9 3          W       E     ♥ 8 7 4
       ♦ K 8 5            S        ♦ 9 7 6 3 2
       ♣ Q 7 3                     ♣ J 10 5
                    ♠ 10 9 3
                    ♥ A Q J 10 6
                    ♦ A Q 10
                    ♣ 4 2
```

West	North	East	South
			1♥
1♠	2♣	pass	2♥
pass	4♥	all pass	

BY THE WAY

Sometimes it takes two ruffs to establish a suit. Suppose you are playing in a major-suit contract with this diamond side suit:

```
          ♦ A K 9 7 3
  ♦ 10 4    N        ♦ Q J 6 2
         W       E
             S
          ♦ 8 5
```

You cash the ace and king and ruff a diamond, finding that the suit breaks 4-2. You enter dummy, by playing some other suit, and ruff another diamond. The thirteenth card in the suit is now good and will be worth a trick.

West scores three spade tricks and switches to a trump. How would you play the contract?

There are no doubt some players at your local club who would rely on the diamond finesse. Bad luck, partner! It's not the only chance, though. After winning the trump switch in your hand you should cash dummy's two top clubs and then ruff a club with one of your high trumps. As it happens, the suit breaks 3-3, so dummy's last two clubs are now good. You have 'established the club suit'. Since trumps break 3-2, you can draw the remaining trumps, ending in the dummy. You can then throw your two potential diamond losers on the established clubs. Suppose the clubs had not broken 3-3, or the trumps had been 4-1. You would have lost nothing by seeking this extra chance. You could still take the diamond finesse.

Let's look at a notrump contract now, where you do not have the option of ruffing when you are trying to establish a suit.

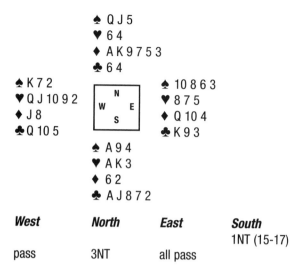

```
                    ♠ Q J 5
                    ♥ 6 4
                    ♦ A K 9 7 5 3
                    ♣ 6 4
        ♠ K 7 2         N          ♠ 10 8 6 3
        ♥ Q J 10 9 2  W   E        ♥ 8 7 5
        ♦ J 8            S          ♦ Q 10 4
        ♣ Q 10 5                    ♣ K 9 3
                    ♠ A 9 4
                    ♥ A K 3
                    ♦ 6 2
                    ♣ A J 8 7 2
```

West	North	East	South
			1NT (15-17)
pass	3NT	all pass	

West leads the ♥Q against 3NT and you win with the ace. What now? The most promising source of tricks is the diamond suit. Suppose you play the ace and king of diamonds, noting the 3-2 break, and continue with a third round of the suit. It will not do you much good! East will win with the ♦Q and knock out your last heart stopper. To gain entry to dummy you will have to play a spade to dummy's queen-jack. West will pounce with the king and cash his heart winners to beat the contract.

As we mentioned a page or two ago, it can work well to duck the first round of a suit that you are trying to establish. See what happens if you play a low diamond from both hands at Trick 2. The defenders win the trick and knock out your second heart stopper. When you play a diamond to the ace, the suit breaks 3-2. The rest of the suit is good and you can cash nine tricks to make your contract.

Even when you are playing in a suit contract, it can be good tactics to duck an early round of the suit that you are planning to establish. Look at this deal:

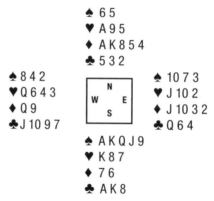

♠ 6 5
♥ A 9 5
♦ A K 8 5 4
♣ 5 3 2

♠ 8 4 2　　　　♠ 10 7 3
♥ Q 6 4 3　　　♥ J 10 2
♦ Q 9　　　　　♦ J 10 3 2
♣ J 10 9 7　　 ♣ Q 6 4

♠ A K Q J 9
♥ K 8 7
♦ 7 6
♣ A K 8

North opens 1♦ and, as South, you bid scientifically to a small slam in spades. How will you play the slam when West leads the ♣J?

You win the club lead and draw trumps. There is a potential loser in both hearts and clubs. The only way to dispose of one or both of these is to set up dummy's diamonds. Suppose you play the ace and king of diamonds and ruff a diamond. All would go sweetly if the suit broke 3-3. You could then cross to the ♥A and discard both your losers, scoring an overtrick. When diamonds break 4-2, which is more likely, life will not be so much fun. You will make only two diamond tricks and go down.

Let's try something different. Suppose you duck a round of diamonds after drawing trumps. You win the heart or club return in the South hand, cross to the ace of diamonds and play the diamond king, discarding a loser. Even when the suit fails to break 3-3, you are still alive! You can ruff a diamond to set up the last card in the suit. You then cross to the ♥A and discard your second loser. 'Nice play, partner!'

Summary

✓ In a suit contract you can establish a long suit by ruffing until the remaining cards become good. By ruffing a round or two, you remove the defenders' high cards.

✓ In notrump you can establish a suit by ducking one or more rounds or by knocking out the defenders' stoppers.

✓ It is sometimes best to duck the first round of a suit that you are trying to establish, leaving the entries in the long holding intact.

ESTABLISHING A SUIT

NOW TRY THESE...

1)

♠ A 4 3
♥ A 5 2
♦ 10 2
♣ K Q 9 6 2

♠ K Q J 10 7 5
♥ 9 6 3
♦ A 3
♣ A 5

West leads the ♥K against 6♠. How will you play the contract? (You will discover that East holds three trumps).

2)

♠ 7 5
♥ 10 6 2
♦ 9 7 3
♣ A 10 7 6 2

♠ A K 8 4
♥ A K 7
♦ A K 5
♣ 8 5 3

West leads the ♦2 against 3NT. How will you play the contract?

3)

♠ 8 5 3
♥ 8 2
♦ A K 7 6 2
♣ 9 7 4

♠ A K 7
♥ A 10 9 3
♦ Q 5 3
♣ A K 8

West leads the ♣Q against 3NT. How will you play?

ANSWERS

1) Win the ♥K lead with dummy's ace. You can count eleven top tricks and must hope for an extra trick from the club suit. You draw two rounds of trumps with the king and queen, West discarding on the second round. You cannot afford to draw East's last trump at this stage because you plan to use dummy's ♠A as an entry. Instead, you play the ace and king of clubs. To guard against a 4-2 break in the suit, you now ruff a club. When you return to dummy with a trump to the ace, drawing East's last trump, you can score the queen and nine of clubs, discarding two of your three red-suit losers. If you make the mistake of drawing three rounds of trumps immediately, you will go down unless clubs happen to break 3-3. You may also go down if you try to cash a third top club, instead of ruffing the third round. When East started with only two clubs, he will ruff the club honor and you will end up two tricks short.

2) You have six top tricks outside clubs and little prospect of any more in those three suits. If you can score three club tricks you will increase your total to nine. Win the diamond lead and duck a round of clubs. Win the diamond return and duck another round of clubs. If the defenders' diamonds break 4-3, as suggested by West's lead of the two, they will not be able to score more than two diamonds at this stage. (The two is West's fourth-best diamond. Since it is the lowest card in the suit, he cannot have a fifth-best diamond!) Provided the club suit breaks 3-2, you will be able to score three club tricks when you win the defenders' return. Because you ducked the first two rounds of clubs, the ♣A remains as an entry to dummy.

3) You can count eight top tricks and the diamond suit will provide two more if it divides 3-2. Suppose you win the club lead and play the queen and ace of diamonds. If East shows out on the second round, the diamond suit breaking 4-1, you will be in trouble. You will have only eight tricks and little prospect of a ninth. To guard against a 4-1 diamond break, you should duck a round of diamonds. You can afford to play the queen on the first round but you should duck the second round. Dummy's ♦A-K-7 will then be good for three tricks, even if the suit breaks 4-1. You give up the possible overtrick (if diamonds break 3-2) in exchange for making the contract when the diamonds break 4-1. A good trade!

C H A P T E R

DISCARDING LOSERS

 When there is no suit in which you are undefended do not be in a hurry to play out winning cards; rather make doubtful cards good. Your winners will not run away, but will come in very useful later on. **W. Dalton.** *Practical Bridge. 1908*

Suppose you are playing in a suit contract and have this side suit:

♣ A K 7

♣ J 9 5 3   N W E S   ♣ 10 8 6 2

♣ Q 4

You can score three club tricks, yes. What may be more important is that you can discard a potential losing card from the South hand on the third round of clubs.

Perhaps the side suit is not ready to cash:

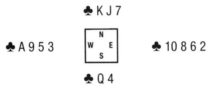

♣ K J 7

♣ A 9 5 3   N W E S   ♣ 10 8 6 2

♣ Q 4

By knocking out the ace of clubs, you can set up two club tricks. Again you will be able to discard a loser from the South hand.

When drawing trumps may involve the defenders gaining the lead (if they hold the ace, for example), your first priority may be to take a discard, or set up a discard. Let's see some deals that will make this clear.

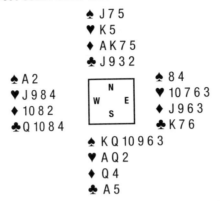

♠ J 7 5
♥ K 5
♦ A K 7 5
♣ J 9 3 2

♠ A 2
♥ J 9 8 4
♦ 10 8 2
♣ Q 10 8 4

♠ 8 4
♥ 10 7 6 3
♦ J 9 6 3
♣ K 7 6

♠ K Q 10 9 6 3
♥ A Q 2
♦ Q 4
♣ A 5

West leads the ♣4 against your small slam in spades, East's king forcing your ace. What now?

Playing a trump doesn't look like a good idea, does it? West will win with the ace and cash a club trick. Your most urgent task is to discard the club loser that West's opening lead has exposed. You should play the queen, ace and king of diamonds, throwing your losing club. Fortunately, diamonds break 4-3 and both defenders follow all the way. With the potential club loser a distant memory, it is safe to play trumps.

Sometimes you must risk a finesse in order to obtain a vital discard. That's the case here:

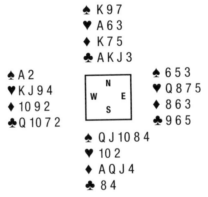

♠ K 9 7
♥ A 6 3
♦ K 7 5
♣ A K J 3

♠ A 2
♥ K J 9 4
♦ 10 9 2
♣ Q 10 7 2

♠ 6 5 3
♥ Q 8 7 5
♦ 8 6 3
♣ 9 6 5

♠ Q J 10 8 4
♥ 10 2
♦ A Q J 4
♣ 8 4

West leads the ♥4 against your small slam in spades. What do you do after winning with dummy's ace?

Playing a trump at Trick 2 would be hopeless. West would win with the ace and have the king of hearts on the table before you could blink. Instead you must seek some way to dispose of your heart loser. The only practical chance is to come to your hand with a top diamond and play a low club to the jack. When the cards lie as in our diagram, the finesse will win. You will then play the ace and king of clubs, discarding your heart loser.

It doesn't happen particularly often but sometimes you can discard a loser from dummy instead of from your own hand. This will enable you to take an eventual ruff in dummy. Look at this deal:

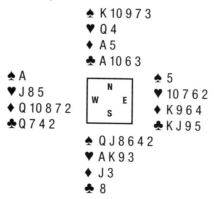

♠ K 10 9 7 3
♥ Q 4
♦ A 5
♣ A 10 6 3

♠ A
♥ J 8 5
♦ Q 10 8 7 2
♣ Q 7 4 2

♠ 5
♥ 10 7 6 2
♦ K 9 6 4
♣ K J 9 5

♠ Q J 8 6 4 2
♥ A K 9 3
♦ J 3
♣ 8

You reach the excellent contract of six spades on this deal and West finds the best lead of a diamond. You win with dummy's ace and once again conclude that playing a trump will be hopeless. Is there any way to discard the losing diamond from your hand? No, there isn't.

How about discarding the losing diamond from dummy? That's a good idea! You play the queen of hearts, followed by the ace and king of hearts. On the third round you discard dummy's ♦5. The sun is now shining. You can start to draw trumps, knowing that the defenders will not be able to score a diamond trick. You will eventually ruff your losing diamond in dummy.

On the next deal, your first priority is to prepare for a discard, rather than to take one immediately :

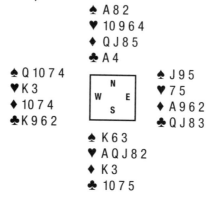

♠ A 8 2
♥ 10 9 6 4
♦ Q J 8 5
♣ A 4

♠ Q 10 7 4
♥ K 3
♦ 10 7 4
♣ K 9 6 2

♠ J 9 5
♥ 7 5
♦ A 9 6 2
♣ Q J 8 3

♠ K 6 3
♥ A Q J 8 2
♦ K 3
♣ 10 7 5

West leads the ♠ 4 against your heart game. How would you play?

Suppose you win with the ace and run the ♥10. The finesse will lose and West will play another spade, setting up a spade trick for the defenders. When you eventually play diamonds, the defenders will win and cash a spade trick. An eventual club loser will put you down.

Setting up a discard on the diamond suit is a higher priority than drawing trumps. Win the spade lead with the king and play the ♦K. If East holds up the ace, play a diamond to the queen. East is welcome to win and knock out the ♠A. You will then throw your spade loser on the ♦J. After this start, you can afford the trump finesse to fail. You will lose one trick each in hearts, diamonds and clubs, making the game comfortably.

Here is a similar deal, where you take a finesse to set up the discard:

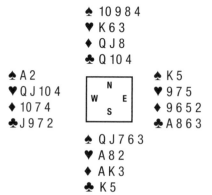

       ♠ 10 9 8 4
       ♥ K 6 3
       ♦ Q J 8
       ♣ Q 10 4

♠ A 2   ♠ K 5
♥ Q J 10 4   ♥ 9 7 5
♦ 10 7 4   ♦ 9 6 5 2
♣ J 9 7 2   ♣ A 8 6 3

       ♠ Q J 7 6 3
       ♥ A 8 2
       ♦ A K 3
       ♣ K 5

West leads the ♥Q against your spade game. It's not difficult to see what will happen if you win and play a trump. The defenders will win and remove your remaining heart stopper, so that you will lose two trumps, one heart and the ace of clubs. What can you do about it?

Before playing a trump, you must seek to establish a discard for your heart loser. Win the heart lead with dummy's king and play a club to the king. When the king wins, play a second club to dummy's ten. This forces the ace, you are pleased to see, and dummy's queen of clubs will now provide a discard. You win the heart return, cross to the queen of diamonds and throw a heart on the queen of clubs. You will draw trumps next, eventually losing just two trumps and a club.

Sometimes you need to establish a long side suit in dummy before a discard can be taken. You will have to play carefully on this next deal:

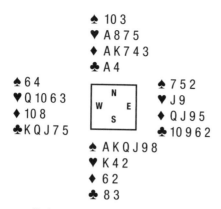

```
                    ♠ 10 3
                    ♥ A 8 7 5
                    ♦ A K 7 4 3
                    ♣ A 4
    ♠ 6 4                          ♠ 7 5 2
    ♥ Q 10 6 3       N             ♥ J 9
    ♦ 10 8        W     E          ♦ Q J 9 5
    ♣ K Q J 7 5      S             ♣ 10 9 6 2
                    ♠ A K Q J 9 8
                    ♥ K 4 2
                    ♦ 6 2
                    ♣ 8 3
```

You reach a small slam in spades and West leads the ♣K, won with dummy's ace. What now?

Suppose you draw trumps before stopping to make a plan. You will go down! You need to discard a heart or a club on dummy's diamond suit. Unless diamonds happen to break 3-3, you will need to ruff two diamonds in order to set up a long card in the suit. One entry to dummy has already gone (the ace of clubs) and you must make full use of the remaining entries, including the ten of trumps. How will you do this?

After winning the club lead with dummy's ace, play the ace and king of diamonds. You then lead a third round of diamonds, ruffing in the South hand. Next you draw two rounds of trumps, crossing to dummy's ten on the second round. A second diamond ruff sets up the thirteenth diamond and you proceed to draw East's last trump. A heart to the ace allows you to discard one of your losers on dummy's good diamond and the slam is yours. As you see, you needed two entries to dummy in addition to those in the diamond suit itself. One was the ten of trumps (to take the second diamond ruff); the other was the ace of hearts (to reach the established diamond).

The need to take a quick discard or two may affect how you play the trump suit itself. Take a look at this deal:

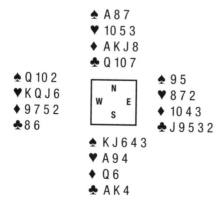

```
                    ♠ A 8 7
                    ♥ 10 5 3
                    ♦ A K J 8
                    ♣ Q 10 7
    ♠ Q 10 2                      ♠ 9 5
    ♥ K Q J 6        N            ♥ 8 7 2
    ♦ 9 7 5 2     W     E         ♦ 10 4 3
    ♣ 8 6            S            ♣ J 9 5 3 2
                    ♠ K J 6 4 3
                    ♥ A 9 4
                    ♦ Q 6
                    ♣ A K 4
```

West leads the ♥K against your small slam in spades and you win with the ace. What now? The normal play with this trump suit is to play the ace and then finesse the jack. If the finesse loses here, West will cash two heart tricks. Perhaps you should play for discards on the diamonds straight away? That's no good. East will ruff the fourth round and you will lose two tricks whether you overruff or not. To make the slam, you must draw two rounds of trumps with the ace and king. You can then play the four diamond winners, discarding both your heart losers. West will score the trump queen but that is all. (If West holds fewer than three diamonds, and ruffs before you can throw both your hearts, there is nothing you can do. You were never going to make this contract.)

Summary

✓ When drawing trumps may result in you losing the lead (for example, when the defenders hold the ace) you may need to take a discard immediately, before playing trumps.

✓ Similarly, when you have two stoppers in the suit led (for example, A-x-x opposite K-x-x), it may be necessary to set up a discard for the loser in this suit before playing trumps and allowing the defenders to remove your remaining stopper.

DISCARDING LOSERS

NOW TRY THESE...

1)

♠ K J 6 2
♥ A 10 7 4
♦ K J 10 5
♣ 7

```
      N
   W     E
      S
```

♠ A 4
♥ 6 5
♦ A Q 4
♣ K Q J 10 9 5

West leads the ♥K against six clubs. How will you play the contract?

2)

♠ K Q 10
♥ 8 7 5 2
♦ K 7 3
♣ K Q 4

```
      N
   W     E
      S
```

♠ A 9 8 6 5 2
♥ Q 9
♦ A 9 2
♣ 8 3

West leads the ♦Q against four spades. How will you play the contract?

3)

♠ A 8 4
♥ Q J 10 6 2
♦ K Q 8 2
♣ 2

```
      N
   W     E
      S
```

♠ J 5
♥ A 9 8 5 3
♦ A 5
♣ K Q J 7

You reach an ambitious small slam in hearts. How should you play when West leads the ♣6?

ANSWERS

1) Suppose you play a trump after winning the first trick with the ace of hearts. That's no good. The defenders will win and cash a heart trick. You must try to discard your heart loser before starting to draw trumps. How about playing four rounds of diamonds? That's no good either. Even if the suit breaks 3-3, one of the defenders will be able to ruff with a low trump. Your only chance is to play the ace of spades followed by a low spade to the jack. If the finesse wins, you can throw a heart on the king of spades. If the finesse loses and the defenders take three tricks, congratulate West on his fine opening lead!

2) If you lose a diamond trick (in addition to two hearts and a club) you will go down. The only way to avoid a diamond loser is to set up a discard on dummy's clubs. Win the diamond lead with the ace and lead a club towards dummy immediately, hoping that West holds the ace. If dummy's king of clubs wins, play the king, queen and ace of trumps. You can then lead a second round of clubs towards dummy's queen. The king of diamonds remains as an entry to cash the club winner, on which you will discard your diamond loser. If you mistakenly play a trump at Trick 2, either the ace or a low trump, you will not have enough entries to your hand to lead towards the clubs twice.

3) Since you have a certain loser in clubs, you need to draw trumps without losing a trick in the suit. After winning the spade lead, you should therefore run the queen of trumps in the hope that East holds the missing king. If the finesse succeeds, you can draw trumps before playing three rounds of diamonds to discard your spade loser. Suppose instead that you play for an immediate discard on the diamonds, before tackling trumps. Whenever the diamond suit breaks 5-2, one of the defenders will ruff the third diamond winner. You will then go down even when the king of trumps is onside.

C H A P T E R 5

THE HOLD-UP
PLAY AT NOTRUMP

 A common type of notrump hand is when you can probably make your contract if you can prevent the original leader's suit from being brought in against you. **W. Dalton.** *Practical Bridge. 1908*

West leads the king of spades against your 3NT contract and this is the layout of the spade suit:

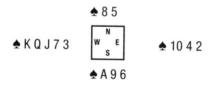

♠ 8 5

♠ K Q J 7 3   ♠ 10 4 2

♠ A 9 6

Most of the time it will be right to **hold up** the spade ace and delay taking it until the third round. What is the point of this? It is to remove all the spades from the East hand. You can then safely lose the lead to East, because he won't have a spade to play. If instead you win the first or second spade, the defenders will be able to cash four spade tricks when East gains the lead.

Let's look at a typical deal where a hold-up will bring home the contract.

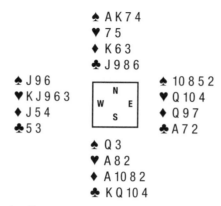

```
              ♠ A K 7 4
              ♥ 7 5
              ♦ K 6 3
              ♣ J 9 8 6
♠ J 9 6                        ♠ 10 8 5 2
♥ K J 9 6 3      N            ♥ Q 10 4
♦ J 5 4       W     E         ♦ Q 9 7
♣ 5 3            S            ♣ A 7 2
              ♠ Q 3
              ♥ A 8 2
              ♦ A 10 8 2
              ♣ K Q 10 4
```

West leads the ♥6 against your contract of 3NT, East playing the queen. How should you aim for nine tricks?

Suppose you win the first round of hearts and play a club. East will win with the ace and return a heart. When the suit breaks 5-3, the defenders will claim four hearts and a club, defeating the game. To cut communications between the defenders you should hold up your ace of hearts until the third round. When you knock out the ace of clubs, East will have no hearts left. You can win whatever else he returns and claim nine tricks for the contract (always an enjoyable moment).

What if West held the ♣A? There was nothing you could do about it in that case. He was destined to score four hearts and the club ace, however smart you were. What if East does have a heart to return when you knock out the club ace? In that case the heart suit was probably divided 4-4 and the defenders can take just three hearts and the ace of clubs.

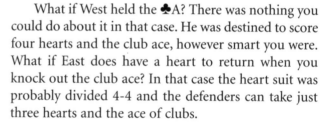

How many rounds should I hold up the ace?

Suppose you are playing in notrump and West leads a club, where you have 10-8-5 in the dummy and A-6-4 in your hand. How many rounds do you need to hold up the ace? You cannot tell from these holdings alone. The answer depends on how the defenders' cards in the suit are split. If West has four clubs and East has three, you will need to hold up twice, to exhaust East's holding in the suit. (This is the purpose of a hold-up play, remember.) If instead West has five clubs and East has two, then you will need to hold up only once. An example deal will make this clear.

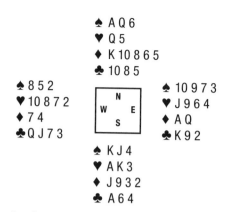

♠ A Q 6
♥ Q 5
♦ K 10 8 6 5
♣ 10 8 5

♠ 8 5 2
♥ 10 8 7 2
♦ 7 4
♣ Q J 7 3

♠ 10 9 7 3
♥ J 9 6 4
♦ A Q
♣ K 9 2

♠ K J 4
♥ A K 3
♦ J 9 3 2
♣ A 6 4

West leads the ♣3 against 3NT, East playing the king. You allow this card to win and East continues with the ♣9. Let's see what happens if you win the second round with the ace. When you run the ♦J, it will lose to the queen. Since East still has a club left, you will lose two diamonds and three clubs, going down one. To make the contract you must hold up twice in clubs. When East wins with the ♦Q, he will then have no club to return. You will win whatever else he plays and knock out the ace of diamonds.

If West's clubs were Q-J-7-3-2, then a single hold-up would be good enough to exhaust East's holding. On this particular deal, you can succeed against either four or five clubs with West by holding up twice.

Sometimes you cannot afford to hold up an ace at all, because you have little or no protection in a different suit. Suppose you are in 3NT with a heart holding of ♥7-2 opposite ♥Q-6. If West fails to lead a heart and tries a spade instead, where you hold ♠10-8-5 opposite ♠A-6-4, a hold-up would be unwise, to put it politely! You would grab your ace and try to score eight quick tricks in the minor suits, before the opponents can switch to hearts.

> **BY THE WAY**
>
> *A good general rule, when your stopper is an ace, is to hold it up twice and win on the third round.*

The hold-up with A-J-x

♠ 4 3 2

♠ 5 led

♠ Q played

♠ A J 6

Whenever you hold A-J-x (what you might call one-and-a-half stoppers) you must think carefully whether to hold up. Your decision will depend on which defender is likely to gain the lead subsequently. If it is the player on your left, you will be inclined to win with the ace immediately, retaining your J-x as a second stopper in the suit. (Your left-hand opponent cannot play spades without setting up your jack.) If the player on your right is likely to gain the lead, taking the ace immediately will not be a good move. Your remaining J-x can be led through and is probably not a second stopper. In that case it would be better to hold up the ace until the third round, hoping to exhaust your right-hand opponent of the suit.

Would you have made the right play here?

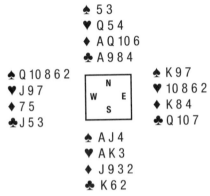

West leads the ♠6 against 3NT and East plays the king. Do you hold up the ace or not?

Which defender might gain the lead on the present deal? Your extra tricks will have to come from diamonds, so East is the defender who may gain the lead. You should therefore hold up the ace of spades for two rounds, winning with it on the third round and then running the ♦J. The diamond finesse loses, as it happens, but since East has no spade to return you will still make the game.

Look back at the diagram and imagine that the North and South diamond holdings are swapped. Now it is West who will gain the lead if the diamond finesse loses. You would therefore win the first round of spades, retaining your ♠J-4 as a second stopper. If the diamond finesse lost to West, he would not be able to play a spade without setting up your jack.

The hold-up with K-Q-x

Suppose you have a holding of K-Q-x and a low card is led to your right-hand opponent's jack or ten. Should you win or hold up? The first point to note is that holding up will not be effective (against competent defenders) when the suit is divided 5-3. Look at this position:

♥ 8 5

♥ A J 9 4 3

♥ 10 7 2

♥ K Q 6

West leads the ♥4 to East's ten. If you hold up, playing the six, East will return the ♥7. When you play one of your honors, West will preserve communications by refusing to win the ace. Now you face the loss of four heart tricks whichever defender gains the lead! So, against a suspected 5-3 break, you must win the first trick and hope to keep East off lead.

When the defenders' suit is divided 6-2 a hold-up may prove effective, because it will exhaust your right-hand opponent of his holding.

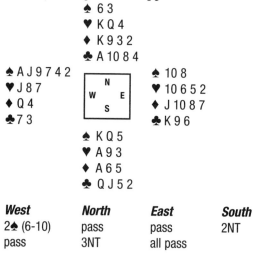

```
              ♠ 6 3
              ♥ K Q 4
              ♦ K 9 3 2
              ♣ A 10 8 4
♠ A J 9 7 4 2            ♠ 10 8
♥ J 8 7         N        ♥ 10 6 5 2
♦ Q 4       W     E      ♦ J 10 8 7
♣ 7 3          S         ♣ K 9 6
              ♠ K Q 5
              ♥ A 9 3
              ♦ A 6 5
              ♣ Q J 5 2
```

West	North	East	South
2♠ (6-10)	pass	pass	2NT
pass	3NT	all pass	

West leads the ♠7 to East's ten. How should you play the contract?

Let's see what happens if you win the first trick. When you take the club finesse, losing to the king, East will have a spade left. His spade return will beat the contract by two tricks. Since East is the defender who will gain the lead if the club finesse happens to fail, you should aim to exhaust his spade holding. You allow East's ♠10 to win the first trick and he returns his last spade. It makes no difference now whether West takes the ace of spades on the second round. Either way, East will have no spade to return when the club finesse loses. You will make the contract.

The hold-up with a double stopper

Even when you have two certain stoppers in the enemy suit, a hold-up can be worthwhile if you may have to lose the lead twice. Look at this deal:

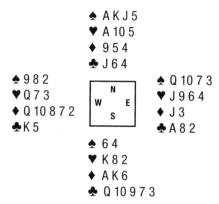

♠ A K J 5
♥ A 10 5
♦ 9 5 4
♣ J 6 4

♠ 9 8 2
♥ Q 7 3
♦ Q 10 8 7 2
♣ K 5

♠ Q 10 7 3
♥ J 9 6 4
♦ J 3
♣ A 8 2

♠ 6 4
♥ K 8 2
♦ A K 6
♣ Q 10 9 7 3

West leads the ♦7 against 3NT and you see you will have to knock out both the ace and king of clubs. Suppose you win the first diamond and lead a club. East will take the first round of clubs with the ace and play another diamond. A hold-up at this stage will be useless. When West gets in with the club king he will play his diamond winners to defeat the game.

Now try holding up at Trick 1. You win the second diamond and play a club. If East takes the first club, he will have no diamond to return. If West wins the first club and clears the diamonds, he will never regain the lead.

Summary

✓ The purpose of a hold-up is to exhaust one defender of the suit led. You can then allow that defender to gain the lead as you set up your own tricks.

✓ When your stopper is an ace, it is usually right to hold it up twice, to be sure of removing all of one opponent's cards in the suit.

✓ With a stopper of A-J-x, consider which defender is likely to gain the lead before deciding whether to hold up.

✓ When the defenders may gain the lead twice as you set up your own tricks, it may be necessary to hold up in their suit even with a double stopper.

THE HOLD-UP PLAY AT NOTRUMP

NOW TRY THESE...

1)

♠ 10 4 3
♥ A J 4
♦ K Q 5
♣ 9 7 6 3

```
      N
  W       E
      S
```

♠ A 8 5
♥ K Q 3
♦ A 10 4
♣ Q J 10 2

East opens the bidding with 1♣. You overcall 1NT and are raised to 3NT. Expecting you to hold strong clubs, West tries the ♠2 as his opening lead. How will you play the contract?

2)

♠ 7 5
♥ Q 6 2
♦ 8 5 3
♣ A J 10 9 6

```
      N
  W       E
      S
```

♠ A J 8
♥ A K 4
♦ A J 9 2
♣ Q 5 3

West leads the ♠4 against 3NT, East playing the ♠K. Will you hold up?

3)

♠ A K 3
♥ K 5
♦ 10 9 7 5 2
♣ 6 4 2

```
      N
  W       E
      S
```

♠ J 7 2
♥ A J 7 3
♦ Q J 3
♣ A Q 8

West leads the ♣5 against 3NT, East playing the ♣K. How will you play?

ANSWERS

1) West's lead of the ♠2 tells you that he has only four spades. (The two is his fourth-best card. He cannot have a fifth-best card because the two is the lowest card in the suit.) Since West holds four spades, East holds three spades. You must therefore hold up the ace of spades for two rounds, to remove East's cards in the suit. It will then be safe to knock out the ace and king of clubs — which East must hold, to make up his opening bid. When East gains the lead he will have no spade to play and you will lose just two spades and two clubs. If you make the mistake of winning the first or second spade, you will go down. You will lose two clubs and (unnecessarily) three spades.

2) When you hold a stopper of A-J-x you must ask yourself which defender is likely to gain the lead. Here you will have to establish the clubs and only East can gain the lead in that suit. If you win the spade ace immediately and take a losing finesse in clubs, a spade return will probably beat you. Instead you should hold up the ace of spades until the third round. If a club finesse loses to East then, he will have no spade to return (or spades will break 4-4 and pose no problem).

3) To score nine tricks you will have to establish the diamonds. Suppose you win East's ♣K with the ace and play a diamond. When clubs break 5-2 and the defenders hold one diamond stopper each, East will win the first round of diamonds and return his remaining club. You have to knock out the other diamond stopper now. West will win and play his winning clubs to beat the game by one trick. Since you have two enemy high cards to dislodge, you should hold up at Trick 1 even though you have a double stopper in clubs. Allow East's ♣K to win the first trick and capture the club return. You will then be safe, provided East holds at least one of the top cards in diamonds. When East takes his diamond trick he will have no club to play.

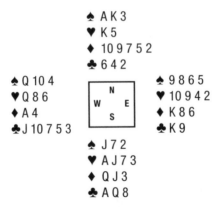

OTHER TYPES OF FINESSE

 It is not always necessary to employ an ace or a king to win a trick; sometimes a card as low as the nine or ten can triumph.
W. Dalton. *Practical Bridge. 1908*

We saw in Chapter 1 that you can give your honor cards the best chance of making a trick by leading towards them. We also looked at the familiar play known as the simple finesse. In this chapter we will look at some further variations of the finesse, which is one of the most useful and important elements of card play.

The double finesse

When you are missing two honors in a suit and take two finesses, this is known as a **double finesse**. Here is a familiar example:

♦ A Q 10

```
┌─────┐
│  N  │
│W   E│
│  S  │
└─────┘
```

♦ 7 6 3

Seeking as many tricks as possible from the suit, you lead a low card from your hand and play dummy's ten. When West holds both the king and jack, the ten will win and you will return to your hand to finesse the queen. Luck is with you and you will score three tricks from the suit.

More often, East will hold one of the missing honors. When he holds the jack, the finesse of the ten will lose but a subsequent finesse of the queen will win. When East holds the king but not the jack, a finesse of the ten will force the king and again give you two tricks. Only when East holds both the missing honors will you fail to score a second trick.

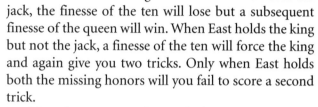

Note that you must finesse the lower card (the ten) on the first round. If you mistakenly began with a successful finesse of the queen, the defenders would still hold the king and jack against you — a subsequent finesse of the ten could not win.

This is a similar combination:

♦ K J 5

```
┌─────┐
│  N  │
│W   E│
│  S  │
└─────┘
```

♦ 7 4 2

Assuming you are trying to make as many tricks as possible, how should you play?

You should lead low to dummy's jack on the first round. If this loses to the queen, you will lead towards the king on the second round. Playing this way, you will score two tricks when West holds both the ace and the queen, one trick when the honors are split (in other words, each defender holds one honor), and no tricks only when East holds the ace and queen.

The next combination offers an apparent guess on the second round:

♣ K 10 9

```
┌─────┐
│  N  │
│W   E│
│  S  │
└─────┘
```

♣ 6 4 3

You hope to make one trick. Playing low to the king on the first round is only a 50% chance. You can do better than that. Lead low to the ten on the first round. This will be an immediate success if West started with both the queen and the jack, since dummy's ten will force East's ace (West does no better to play an honor). Much of the time the ten will lose to East's queen or jack. On the second round you should then finesse the nine. Playing in this fashion, you will score a trick more than 75% of the time — when West holds either the queen or jack, and also when he holds a doubleton ace. Rising with the king on the second round is not such a good play. You would score a second trick only about 62% of the time (when West holds the queen *and* jack or when he holds the ace).

Sometimes a double finesse position offers a choice of plays on the first round. How would you play this spade suit for two tricks?

♠ Q 10 9

```
    N
  W   E
    S
```

♠ A 6 2

Suppose you play the ace and lead a low card towards dummy. If West holds both missing honors, you cannot go wrong; if East holds them, you will score only the ace. What if the missing honors are split — West and East each have one? Unless you are incredibly lucky and an honor appears from West, you will have a 50% guess to make a second trick. So your total prospects of taking two tricks, playing this way, are just a little over 50%.

A better idea is to take a **double finesse**, leading the queen from dummy on the first round. If East holds the king you will score two spade tricks, whether or not he covers. If you are unlucky on the first round, West winning with the king, you can run the ten on the next round. You will fail in your mission only when West holds both honors. This line increases your chances of taking two tricks to a little over 75%. A considerable improvement.

Strangely, your prospects are exactly the same if you replace dummy's queen with the jack:

♠ J 10 9

```
    N
  W   E
    S
```

♠ A 6 2

You run the jack on the first round. If this loses, you run the ten on the second round. Once again you will score a second trick unless West holds both the missing honors.

Here is something a bit different:

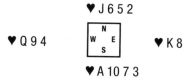

♥ J 6 5 2

♥ Q 9 4
```
    N
  W   E
    S
```
    ♥ K 8

♥ A 10 7 3

Aiming for three tricks, you play low to the ten on the first round. This will be an immediate success if East started with K-Q-x. Either the ten will win or East will have to split his honors. But you also make three tricks when East holds a doubleton honor, as in the diagram. The ten loses to the queen but the ace drops the king on the second round, promoting dummy's jack.

Suppose, for some reason, that you think West (rather than East) holds only two hearts. For example, West may have shown a long suit elsewhere and is therefore likely to be shorter in hearts. This may be the position:

♥ J 6 5 2

♥ Q 8   ♥ K 9 4

♥ A 10 7 3

To score three heart tricks now you must lead a low heart from the South hand on the first round. If West rises with his doubleton honor (as most of the world's defenders will), you can finesse against East on the second round. If West chooses to play low, and you read the situation, you can drop his queen with the ace on the next round.

The deep finesse

What do you make of this holding?

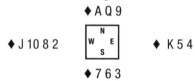

♦ A Q 9

♦ J 10 8 2   ♦ K 5 4

♦ 7 6 3

Seeking two tricks, you should lead low to the nine on the first round. This is called a **deep finesse**, because the defenders hold three cards higher than the card you are finessing. When West holds both the jack and the ten, dummy's nine will force the king and you will score two tricks. (It would make no difference if West inserted the jack or ten. This would be covered by the queen and king and you would subsequently finesse dummy's nine.) If instead the nine loses to the jack or ten with East, you have lost nothing. You can finesse the queen on the next round.

This is a similar position:

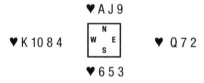

♥ A J 9

♥ K 10 8 4   ♥ Q 7 2

♥ 6 5 3

If you lead low to dummy's jack, you will succeed only when West holds both the king and the queen. A better idea is to take a deep finesse of the nine on the first round. When West's holding is headed by either K-10 or Q-10, the nine will force a high honor and set up a successful finesse of the jack on the next round.

The deep finesse is very common and merits a third example:

You play low to the ten on the first round, forcing East's ace. You can then lead towards dummy's queen, establishing a trick in the suit.

Let's see a whole deal that features a deep finesse:

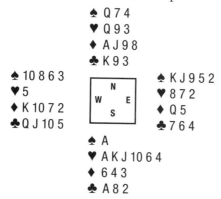

West leads the ♣Q against your ambitious small slam in hearts. You have two potential losers in diamonds and one in clubs. You must aim to play the diamonds so that you not only restrict your losers to one in that suit, but also set up a discard for the losing club.

You win the club lead with the ace and draw trumps in three rounds, ending in your hand. Hoping that West's diamonds are headed by the K-10 or Q-10 (or K-Q-10), you next lead a low diamond to dummy's nine. The signs are promising when East wins with the queen. You win the club return with the king, cross to the ace of spades, and play a diamond to dummy's eight. When it wins the trick, you know you will make the contract. You return to the South hand with a spade ruff and lead a third round of diamonds to dummy's jack, East showing out. You discard your club loser on the ace of diamonds and the slam is yours.

The backwards finesse

Sometimes the opponents' bidding lets you know that a simple finesse against a queen is destined to fail. In such a situation a maneuver known as the **backwards finesse** may be possible. Look at this deal:

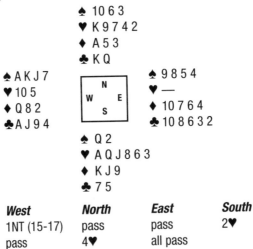

♠ 10 6 3
♥ K 9 7 4 2
♦ A 5 3
♣ K Q

♠ A K J 7
♥ 10 5
♦ Q 8 2
♣ A J 9 4

♠ 9 8 5 4
♥ —
♦ 10 7 6 4
♣ 10 8 6 3 2

♠ Q 2
♥ A Q J 8 6 3
♦ K J 9
♣ 7 5

West	North	East	South
1NT (15-17)	pass	pass	2♥
pass	4♥	all pass	

You reach game in hearts after West has opened a 15-17 point 1NT. West plays the two top spades, followed by the ace of clubs and the jack of spades, to kill dummy's ten. You ruff the third round of spades. How should you continue?

Since you can see twenty-five points between your own hand and the dummy, West is marked with every missing honor card. In particular, he will hold the ♦Q and a straightforward finesse of the diamond jack is therefore destined to fail. What else can you try?

After drawing trumps, you should lead the ♦J from your hand. If West declines to cover, you will run the jack and claim the remaining tricks. If instead West covers with the queen, you will win with dummy's ace of diamonds. Your ♦K-9 will then lie over East's ♦10-7. You can lead a low diamond from dummy and finesse the nine.

The ruffing finesse

Finally, let's look at something quite different, the ruffing finesse:

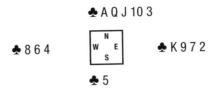

♣ A Q J 10 3

♣ 8 6 4

♣ K 9 7 2

♣ 5

If this is a side suit in a suit contract, you can catch East's ♣K with a **ruffing finesse**. You cash the ace and then lead the queen. If East covers with the king, you will ruff. Otherwise you will discard a loser and continue to lead dummy's honors until East plays the king. Should the ruffing finesse lose to the king with West, the remainder of the suit will provide discards.

A ruffing finesse is the best play on this deal:

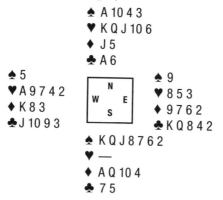

```
                    ♠ A 10 4 3
                    ♥ K Q J 10 6
                    ♦ J 5
                    ♣ A 6
    ♠ 5                         ♠ 9
    ♥ A 9 7 4 2      N          ♥ 8 5 3
    ♦ K 8 3      W     E        ♦ 9 7 6 2
    ♣ J 10 9 3       S          ♣ K Q 8 4 2
                    ♠ K Q J 8 7 6 2
                    ♥ —
                    ♦ A Q 10 4
                    ♣ 7 5
```

West leads the ♣J against your small slam in spades and you win with the ace in dummy. How should you play the contract?

You have one club loser and a potential second loser in diamonds. Suppose you draw trumps and take the diamond finesse, running the jack. If East holds the diamond king, you will not only avoid a diamond loser, you will also set up a discard for dummy's club loser. You can then ruff a club in dummy and score an overtrick. But what if you are unlucky and the diamond finesse loses? When West wins with the diamond king he will play another club and you will go down.

There is a much better line of play available — a ruffing finesse in hearts. After drawing trumps, you lead the king of hearts from dummy. Here East will play low and you will discard your club loser. The ruffing finesse loses to West's ace but you don't mind at all! Dummy's remaining Q-J-10 in the heart suit will allow you to throw away three diamonds and you will make the slam. If East had held the ace of hearts, playing it on dummy's king, you would ruff in the South hand. Again the remaining hearts in dummy would provide three discards (four discards if the heart suit happened to divide 4-4).

So, the simple diamond finesse gives you a 50% chance of making the slam. The ruffing heart finesse gives you a 100% chance. The choice is yours!

Summary

✓ When a combination offers the chance of taking two finesses, for example: A-Q-10 opposite x-x-x, finesse the lower card first. If the ten loses to the jack, you will finesse the queen next. Such a position is known as a **double finesse**.

✓ With A-Q-9 opposite x-x-x, do not finesse the queen on the first round. If you finesse the nine first, you give yourself the extra chance that this will force the king. This play is known as a **deep finesse**.

✓ When you hold a sequence of honors opposite a singleton or void, you may be able to execute a **ruffing finesse**. For example, with A-Q-J-7 opposite a singleton, you can play the ace and lead the queen on the next round. If the second player covers with the king, you will ruff. If he does not cover, you will discard a loser.

OTHER TYPES OF FINESSE

NOW TRY THESE...

1)

♠ Q 7 2
♥ A 8 6 3
♦ A J 10
♣ K 8 6

```
      N
  W       E
      S
```

♠ A K 6
♥ K Q 4
♦ 7 6 2
♣ A Q J 5

West leads the ♠J against 6NT. How will you play the contract?

2)

♠ A J 7 5
♥ 7 5 3
♦ A 9 5
♣ K 8 3

```
      N
  W       E
      S
```

♠ Q 8 6 3 2
♥ A Q 10
♦ 7 4 2
♣ A 6

West leads the ♣J against four spades. How will you play the contract?

3)

♠ A 5 2
♥ A Q J 6
♦ 9 7 4
♣ K 8 3

```
      N
  W       E
      S
```

♠ K Q J 10 7 6 3
♥ 7
♦ A 8
♣ A 10 5

West leads the ♦K against six spades. How will you play the contract?

ANSWERS

1) You have eleven top tricks and must seek one more. A 3-3 heart break will give you an extra trick. So will a successful double finesse in diamonds. You can combine these chances provided you take the first diamond finesse before testing the hearts. Win the spade lead with the ace and play a diamond to the jack. Assuming this loses to the king or queen, win East's return and test the heart suit. If it fails to divide 3-3, return to the South hand and take another diamond finesse.

2) You have five potential losers: one in spades and two in each red suit. You must first attempt to draw trumps without losing a trick. Win the club lead with the ace and lead a low trump (not the queen, since this would cost a trick if West held a singleton king). If a finesse of dummy's jack of trumps succeeds, play the ace next, hoping that trumps break 2-2. Whether or not you manage to escape a trump loser, you will take a double finesse in the heart suit. To give yourself a chance of three heart tricks — which is vital if you have lost a trump trick — you must finesse the ten of hearts on the first round, finessing the queen on the next round if necessary. If you manage to avoid a trump loser, you will need at least one of the heart honors to be onside. If you lose a trump trick, you will need both heart honors to be onside.

3) You win the diamond lead and draw trumps. You would like to discard your diamond loser. Suppose you lead a low heart to dummy's queen and this wins the trick. You can then discard your diamond loser on dummy's ace of hearts. Will this draw a 'Well played, partner!' from across the table, do you think? It shouldn't, because if the heart finesse had lost you would have gone down. The safe way to play the slam is to take a ruffing finesse in hearts. You play a heart to the ace and lead dummy's queen. If the king appears from East, you will ruff in the South hand. You can then return to dummy with a club to throw your diamond loser on the established jack of hearts. If instead the heart king does not appear from East, you will discard your diamond loser. You don't mind at all if the ruffing finesse loses to West's king. Dummy's jack of hearts will be established and you can discard your club loser on it.

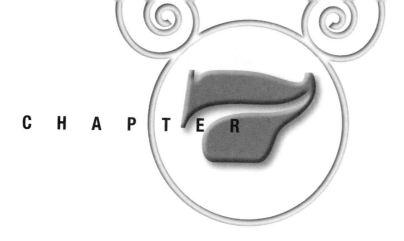

C H A P T E R 7

SAFETY PLAYS
WITHIN ONE SUIT

Even within a single suit, there are many hundreds of card combinations possible. It is not practical to learn all the 'best plays' and you will often have to work them out at the table. How do you do this? Let's look at a typical holding:

♠ A K J 4

♠ ?   ♠ ?

♠ 8 5 2

A bridge colleague of yours shows you this suit, scribbled on the back of an old scorecard. 'What is the best play here?' you are asked. What should your reply be?

You cannot give an answer unless you know how many tricks you need from the suit. Suppose you need all four spade tricks to make the contract. You would have to finesse the jack, hoping that West started with Q-x-x. Suppose instead that you need only three spade tricks. What would be the best play then?

If you made the same play — finessing the jack — you would fail to make three tricks when East started with a doubleton queen in the suit. To give yourself the best chance of three tricks, you should play the ace and king first (possibly dropping a doubleton queen with East). If the queen does not fall, you will return to the South hand in a different suit and lead towards the jack of spades on the third round. If West holds the queen, or the suit breaks 3-3, you will make the required three spade tricks.

That was a typical 'safety play'. You played as safely as possible to make the required number of tricks. There was a small price to be paid: you would not make four spade tricks when West held Q-x-x in the suit. That is true of many safety plays: you surrender a possible overtrick in order to give yourself the best possible chance of making the contract.

Here is a similar combination for you to try.

♣ Q 6 3 2

♣ ?   ♣ ?

♣ A 7 4

If you need three club tricks you should lead low to the queen, hoping that West holds K-x-x (it makes little difference if you play the ace first).

Suppose you need only two club tricks. What then? All will be easy when the suit breaks 3-3 or West holds the ♣K. There is nothing you can do when East holds four clubs including the king. What if East holds K-x? Yes, you can improve your chances of two tricks by cashing the ace and then ducking a round. When the king is doubleton, it will appear on the second round. If it doesn't, you can return to hand and lead towards the club queen on the third round, still making the required two tricks when West holds the ♣K.

How would you tackle this combination?

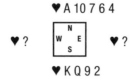

♥ A 10 7 6 4

♥ ?   ♥ ?

♥ K Q 9 2

You reach a grand slam in hearts and note that you will go down only if you lose a trump trick. What is the safety play to avoid such a loss?

When you are missing four cards to the jack you must aim to keep a high card over the jack, whichever defender has all four cards. You do this by cashing an honor from the hand with two honors — here you will start with the king (or queen). If West holds J-x-x-x, you will finesse dummy's ten on the second round. If East holds J-x-x-x, you will cross to the ace and finesse the nine.

Most players get that one right but they may falter on the next combination, which is confusingly similar. How would you play this spade suit to give yourself the best chance of five tricks?

♠ A K 9 7 3

♠ ?　　N W E S　　♠ ?

♠ Q 8 6 2

If you start with the ace or king, you will not succeed against J-10-x-x in either hand! To pick up such a holding, you need to have two higher honors over the jack and ten. You should therefore first play the honor in the hand that contains only one honor (the queen, here). If West started with J-10-x-x, you can now score all five tricks. You lead towards the A-K-9 on the second round, planning to finesse the nine. If West prevents this by playing one of his honors — 'splitting his honors', as it is called — you will win the trick and return to the South hand to finesse against his remaining honor. (If East started with J-10-x-x, there is nothing you can do about it.)

How would you play this suit?

♦ A J 6 2

♦ ?　　N W E S　　♦ ?

♦ K 9 5 3

Once again, the correct answer is: 'How many tricks do I need from the suit?' If you need all four diamond tricks, you do best to finesse the jack on the first round. You need West to hold one, two or three cards including the queen.

Suppose you need only three diamond tricks. Is there a play that succeeds against Q-10-x-x with either defender? Suppose you start the same way — finessing the jack, which loses to the queen. If you play the king next, you will lose two tricks when East has Q-10-x-x. If instead you play the ace next, you will lose two tricks when East's ♦Q was a singleton.

Perhaps you should start with a low card to the nine, intending to play the king next? No, you would lose two tricks when West started with a singleton ten. The best play is to cash the ace first and then lead a second round towards the nine. If East follows, you finesse the nine. Either the finesse will win, West showing out, or the suit will break 3-2. In both cases you will score the three tricks you need. Suppose next that East shows out on the second round. You simply rise with the king and lead back towards the jack. This is a 100% safety play for three tricks against a 4-1 break.

As you see, it can be quite arduous to work out the best play. Experienced players would be familiar with that last combination and would know straight away how to play the suit.

BY THE WAY

Do you see why it is wrong to play the king first? If East holds a single queen, you cannot score four tricks anyway. If West holds a single queen, you must play low to West's queen and dummy's ace, cashing the jack next and then finessing the nine.

The safety play on the next combination is perhaps easier to calculate:

♠ A 9 6 2

♠ ?   ♠ ?

♠ K 10 7 5 4

You are playing in six spades and have no losers in the side suits. How will you give yourself the best chance of avoiding two trump losers?

Suppose you play a low card to the ace. You will lose two trump tricks when West started with Q-J-x-x. A low card to the king is just the same. If West shows out, you will lose two trump tricks. Let's try playing low to the nine instead. If East wins with the queen or jack, the suit will have broken 3-1 at worst, so there will be only one loser. If West started with all four trumps, the nine will win on the first round. What if West shows out when you lead low towards dummy? You can either finesse the nine, losing to East, and finesse the ten later. Or you can rise with the ace and lead low to the ten on the second round, forcing East to split his honors. (Leading a low card to the ten on the first round is just as good, of course.)

'I may lose an unnecessary trick if the spade suit breaks 2-2,' you may be thinking. It's perfectly true, but trumps will break 4-0 every now and again and it is more important to guarantee the slam than to chase an extra 30 points!

Summary

✓ Calculate the best play in a suit by seeing how many lies of the defenders' cards each particular play will succeed against.

✓ Often the safe way of playing a suit will give up the chance of an overtrick. Don't worry about that. It's a good investment.

SAFETY PLAYS WITHIN ONE SUIT

NOW TRY THESE...

1)

♠ A J 7 4

```
    N
 W     E
    S
```

♠ K 5 2

How do you give yourself the best chance of three spade tricks?

2)

♥ Q 9 5 3 2

```
    N
 W     E
    S
```

♥ K J 8 4

How do you play this suit to guarantee four tricks?

3)

♦ J 7 2

```
    N
 W     E
    S
```

♦ A K 6 4

What is the best play to make three diamond tricks?

4)

♣ K 9 7 6 2

```
    N
 W     E
    S
```

♣ 10 8 5 3

How do you play this suit if you need (a) four tricks, or (b) three tricks?

5)

♠ A 10 6 4

```
    N
 W     E
    S
```

♠ K 7 5 2

How do you play this suit as safely as possible for three tricks?

ANSWERS

1) You start by cashing the ace and the king, picking up a possible Q-x with East. If the queen does not fall, lead towards the jack on the third round. You make the required three tricks if West holds the queen, if East holds a singleton or doubleton queen, or if the suit breaks 3-3.

2) You can score four tricks when either defender holds A-10-x-x. provided you play the king or jack on the first round. If a defender shows up with A-10-x-x, you will finesse against his ten on the second round.

3) You should start by playing the ace, in case the queen is singleton. What should you do next — cash the king or play low to the jack? If West started with Q-x, or the suit breaks 3-3, both plays will work. Cashing the king will succeed when East started with Q-x; playing low to the jack will succeed when West started with Q-x-x-x. Which is more likely? It is twice as likely that West holds Q-x-x-x than that East has Q-x. That's because when a suit breaks 4-2 the player with four cards is twice as likely to hold a particular card as the player with only two. You should therefore lead towards the jack on the second round. (Note that if East has Q-x-x-x; it doesn't matter what you do — you will only make two diamond tricks.)

4) You can make four tricks only when West holds a doubleton ace. So, lead low to the king on the first round. When you need only three tricks, duck the first round and lead towards the king on the second round. This will prevent you from losing three tricks when East has a singleton ace.

5) If East holds any four cards in the suit, he is bound to take two tricks. You should therefore concentrate on the situation where West holds four cards. Play the king first and lead low towards the ten. If West follows low, you can guarantee three tricks by finessing the ten. If instead West splits his honors, you can either duck (intending to finesse on the next round if East shows out) or you can win with the ace and return to the South hand to lead towards dummy's ten.

HOW TO PLAN A NOTRUMP CONTRACT

 You will very likely be obliged to change your tactics as the game develops, but from the first start of the hand you should always have a plan of campaign in your head.
W. Dalton. *Practical Bridge. 1908*

What is the first thing you do when the opening lead is made against your notrump contract and the dummy goes down? If you are like us, you will probably look to see if you have a stopper in the suit led! After that, you must make a plan. The first step is to count how many **top tricks** you have. What does 'top tricks' mean? It means tricks that are ready to cash. With ♣K-Q-J-2 opposite ♣10-9-7, for example, you would have no top tricks in clubs. You would have to knock out the defenders' ace before you could score any tricks in the suit. Having counted your top tricks, you must then look for the safest way to establish the extra tricks you need to make the contract.

Let's go through this process on a relatively simple deal:

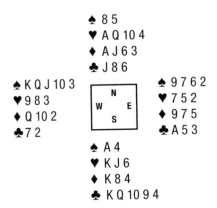

♠ 8 5
♥ A Q 10 4
♦ A J 6 3
♣ J 8 6

♠ K Q J 10 3   ♠ 9 7 6 2
♥ 9 8 3   ♥ 7 5 2
♦ Q 10 2   ♦ 9 7 5
♣ 7 2   ♣ A 5 3

♠ A 4
♥ K J 6
♦ K 8 4
♣ K Q 10 9 4

West leads the ♠K against 3NT. How would you plan the play?

You can count seven top tricks (one spade, four hearts and two diamonds). You need two extra tricks to make your game. By knocking out the ace of clubs you can establish four extra tricks. You must ask yourself: is it safe to establish the clubs? No! The defenders will win and score at least four spades and the club ace. You look next at the diamonds. Can that suit yield the two extra tricks that you need? Yes, but only if the defenders' cards lie in a particular way. If West holds the queen and the suit divides 3-3, a finesse of the diamond jack will give you four diamond tricks. It's not very likely, but some chance is better than none and you should therefore try for four diamond tricks. On this occasion, the play brings home the game.

Let's change that last deal slightly:

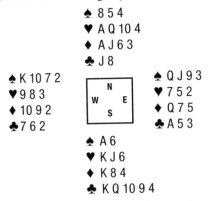

♠ 8 5 4
♥ A Q 10 4
♦ A J 6 3
♣ J 8

♠ K 10 7 2   ♠ Q J 9 3
♥ 9 8 3   ♥ 7 5 2
♦ 10 9 2   ♦ Q 7 5
♣ 7 6 2   ♣ A 5 3

♠ A 6
♥ K J 6
♦ K 8 4
♣ K Q 10 9 4

This time West leads the ♠2 against 3NT. What is your plan now?

As we have seen before, the lead of a fourth-best two of spades tells you that the spades are breaking 4-4. In that case it will be safe to knock out the ace of clubs. (You will lose only three spades and one club.)

Seeking reassurance, you duck the first round of spades. East wins with the jack and returns the ♠3. Since it is customary to return the fourth-best card from an original holding of four or more, East's play confirms that spades are 4-4. Even if your opponents are the trickiest customers on earth, it is surely more likely that spades are 4-4 after this start than to find West with Q-x-x in diamonds. You win the second spade and put your card reading to the test by boldly playing a club. Spades are indeed 4-4, so the defenders score just two more tricks in the suit and you make your game. Had you taken the diamond finesse instead, you would have gone down. The defenders would have made three spades, a diamond and a club.

Let's see a deal now where you have to establish one suit or another and must choose which one to attack.

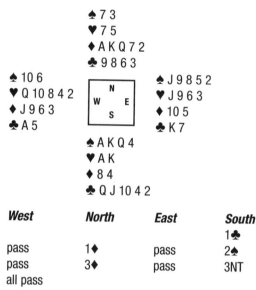

West	North	East	South
			1♣
pass	1♦	pass	2♠
pass	3♦	pass	3NT
all pass			

West leads the ♥4 to East's jack and your king. What is your plan?

You have eight top tricks and therefore need one more trick for game. Do you have time to knock out the two club stoppers? No, because the defenders will score two clubs and at least three hearts before you can take nine tricks yourself. So, you must rely on the diamond suit to provide the extra trick you need. The best play there, as we saw in Chapter 3, is to duck the first round of diamonds — playing a low diamond from both hands. You win the heart return and cross to dummy with a diamond to the ace. When both defenders follow to the second round, the contract is secure. You score three spades, two hearts and four diamonds.

For our final example, we will look at a lowly 1NT contract:

BY THE WAY

Suppose on this deal that your spades were not as good, just ♠A-K-8-4. You would then have only seven top tricks. Needing a full five tricks from the diamond suit, you would have to hope for a 3-3 diamond break. You would play the diamond suit from the top, cashing the three honors.

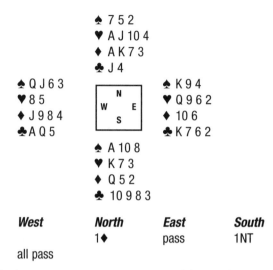

♠ 7 5 2
♥ A J 10 4
♦ A K 7 3
♣ J 4

♠ Q J 6 3
♥ 8 5
♦ J 9 8 4
♣ A Q 5

♠ K 9 4
♥ Q 9 6 2
♦ 10 6
♣ K 7 6 2

♠ A 10 8
♥ K 7 3
♦ Q 5 2
♣ 10 9 8 3

West	North	East	South
	1♦	pass	1NT
all pass			

West leads the ♠3 against 1NT. How would you plan the play?

The first point to note is that West's ♠3 lead (when you can see the ♠2) tells you he has only four spades. You have six top tricks and need only one more. A 3-3 break in diamonds would be good enough. Should you play three rounds of that suit first? Certainly not! If the diamonds failed to break 3-3 you would set up an extra trick for the defenders (West's ♦J) — enough to put you down when added to three tricks in each black suit.

A successful finesse in hearts would also give you a seventh trick. Perhaps that is the best move? No, this play suffers from the same defect. If the finesse loses, you will set up a seventh trick for the defenders. The best line is to win the spade lead and develop the club suit. The defenders are welcome to their three tricks in this suit. You will set up a club winner on the fourth round and this will be your (safe) seventh trick.

Summary

✓ To plan a notrump contract, count your top tricks and look for the safest way to increase this total to the required number.

✓ The best play may depend on how the defenders' main suit is breaking. Look carefully at the spot card led, and at any cards that the defenders play subsequently in that suit. You can usually tell whether the suit is divided 4-4 or 5-3.

HOW TO PLAN A NOTRUMP CONTRACT

1)

♠ 8 7
♥ K 3
♦ Q 7 6 3
♣ J 10 8 6 2

```
      N
  W       E
      S
```

♠ A K
♥ A Q J 4
♦ K J 2
♣ Q 9 7 4

West leads the ♣4 against 3NT. Plan the play.

2)

♠ A Q
♥ K 9 4
♦ Q 6 3
♣ A J 9 6 4

```
      N
  W       E
      S
```

♠ J 8 6 4
♥ A 7 3
♦ A 7
♣ Q 10 7 3

West leads the ♦5 against 3NT. Plan the play. (Will you play dummy's queen of diamonds at Trick 1?)

3)

♠ 9 3
♥ A Q 10
♦ A J 7 6 3
♣ Q 8 3

```
      N
  W       E
      S
```

♠ A K
♥ 7 6 2
♦ Q 10 9 5 2
♣ K J 4

West leads the ♠4 against 3NT. Plan the play. (You will need two separate plans, depending on which defender holds the ♦K.)

ANSWERS

1) You have six top tricks and must seek three more in order to make the contract. How about playing clubs? By knocking out the ace and king of clubs, you can set up three extra tricks in the suit — enough for the contract. However, the defenders will beat you to the finish line. They will set up their spade suit when you knock out the first club stopper. When they take their second club trick they will be able to take at least six tricks: three spades, two clubs and a diamond. That's no good. Instead you should knock out the ace of diamonds, hoping that this suit breaks 3-3. As we saw before, even a slim chance is better than none!

2) You have five top tricks. If West holds the king of clubs, you can score four extra tricks from the club suit and make the game easily. You must therefore concentrate your thoughts on what will happen when East has the club king. You will then need a second diamond stopper. It follows that you should not play dummy's ♦Q at Trick 1. This would put the contract at risk if East happened to hold the ♦K. Win the first trick with the diamond ace and run the queen of clubs. If the finesse loses, East cannot play a diamond without setting up dummy's ♦Q and giving you your ninth trick. Nor can he damage you with any other return. Say he plays a heart. You win with the ace and finesse the spade queen. You don't mind this finesse losing either. Dummy's queen still protects the diamond suit. Meanwhile your ♠J will be good for a ninth trick.

3) You can count four top tricks. Win the spade lead and take the diamond finesse. If it wins, you will have eight tricks and can afford to knock out the ace of clubs to set up two more tricks there. Suppose the diamond finesse loses and East clears the spade suit. You cannot afford to play clubs now because the defenders would score at least three spades, the diamond king and the ace of clubs. Instead you have to hope that West holds both the king and the jack of hearts. Finesse the ten of hearts, return to the South hand and finesse the queen of hearts. Only a 1-in-4 chance, yes, but that is better than none!

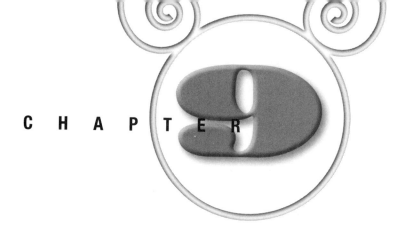

C H A P T E R

HOW TO PLAN A
⌐SUIT CONTRACT⌐

 Do not be in a hurry to play to the first trick, but wait a few moments and review your forces.
W. Dalton. *Practical Bridge. 1908*

In the last chapter we saw how to plan a notrump contract. Basically, you count how many top tricks you have and look for the safest way to increase this to the required total. When playing in a suit contract, most players find it easier to use a different method — to count the 'possible losers' in the hand with the longer trumps and to seek the safest way to reduce this total to the required number.

What do we mean by 'possible losers'? The easiest way to explain this is with a sample deal:

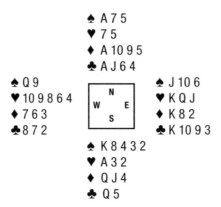

```
              ♠ A 7 5
              ♥ 7 5
              ♦ A 10 9 5
              ♣ A J 6 4
♠ Q 9                      ♠ J 10 6
♥ 10 9 8 6 4               ♥ K Q J
♦ 7 6 3                    ♦ K 8 2
♣ 8 7 2                    ♣ K 10 9 3
              ♠ K 8 4 3 2
              ♥ A 3 2
              ♦ Q J 4
              ♣ Q 5
```

West leads the ♥10 against four spades, East playing the jack. The first stage in planning a suit contract is to count the possible losers in the long-trump hand (South, here). You have at least one loser in the trump suit, two more in hearts, and a possible further loser in each minor. So, 'loser' simply means a trick that you might lose. Assuming that the trumps do break 3-2, you have five losers in your hand and must seek to reduce this total to three — the most you can afford in a major-suit game.

Look at each suit in turn. In the trump suit there is nothing you can do. You must hope for a 3-2 break, which will restrict the trump losers to one. In hearts you have two potential losers. You note that if you give up a heart trick before drawing trumps you will be able to ruff a heart, reducing the losers in the suit to one. To avoid a diamond loser you could try a finesse in the suit. In clubs you could also take a finesse, but you are not inclined to do so because the diamond suit will provide a discard for your club loser, whether or not the diamond finesse succeeds.

You now make a plan: 'I will duck a heart, so that I can ruff a heart in dummy. After drawing trumps, I will finesse in diamonds. Even if this loses, I will then have a discard for my club loser.'

How does the play go? You allow East's jack of hearts to win the first trick. Let's say he plays another heart. You win with the ace, ruff a heart and then play the ace and king of trumps. The suit breaks 3-2. Good! You run the queen of diamonds and this loses to East. Whatever he returns, you will discard your potential club loser on the fourth round of diamonds to make the game.

Your plan on that deal made use of the three main ways to dispose of potential losers:

> • *ruffing*
> • *finessing*
> • *discarding*

You ruffed a heart, avoiding one of your losers in that suit. You finessed in diamonds, hoping to avoid a loser there if the finesse were to win. Finally, you discarded a club loser on the established long card in diamonds. By avoiding the potential loser in clubs and one of the two heart losers, you reduced the count of possible losers from five to three.

When it came to avoiding a club loser you might have used either finessing or discarding. Since a finesse would involve some risk and taking a discard would not, it was obvious to choose the discard.

Let's look at another deal and this time try to identify the losers yourself. You must then decide which of the three methods, if any, are appropriate to reduce the losers in each suit. Finally, you must construct a plan for the play.

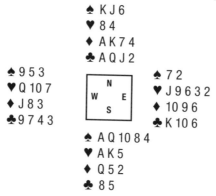

♠ K J 6
♥ 8 4
♦ A K 7 4
♣ A Q J 2

♠ 9 5 3
♥ Q 10 7
♦ J 8 3
♣ 9 7 4 3

♠ 7 2
♥ J 9 6 3 2
♦ 10 9 6
♣ K 10 6

♠ A Q 10 8 4
♥ A K 5
♦ Q 5 2
♣ 8 5

Feeling adventurous, you bid to a grand slam in spades. West leads a trump and down goes the dummy. How will you plan the play?

Look at the losers in the hand with the longer trumps (South). There are no trump losers, one potential loser in hearts, no diamond losers and one potential loser in clubs. How can you dispose of your heart loser? By ruffing it in dummy. How can you dispose of the club loser? One possibility is to take a club finesse. Do you see any other chance? If diamonds break 3-3, you can throw your club loser on the fourth round of diamonds.

Since you need a heart ruff, it would be a mistake to draw all the trumps straight away. You can draw one more round of trumps, cash the two heart winners and ruff the ♥5 in the dummy. You then cross to the diamond queen and draw West's remaining trump. Before relying on a club finesse, you should test the diamond suit by playing the ace and king. When the cards lie as in the diagram, you're in luck! Diamonds break 3-3 and you can throw a club on the fourth round of diamonds. If the diamonds had not broken 3-3, you would have returned to the South hand by ruffing dummy's fourth diamond. Hoping for the best, you would then have to take a club finesse.

BY THE WAY

To 'test a suit' means to play a few rounds, to discover how the defenders' cards lie. On this deal you test the diamonds by playing the ace, king and queen.

From these two example deals you can see that a good declarer does not like to rely on a finesse before exhausting all the other possibilities. (If you like taking unnecessary risks, perhaps you should play roulette instead of bridge!)

We have space for one more deal. Once again you must count the losers in each suit and plan how to reduce the total to the required number.

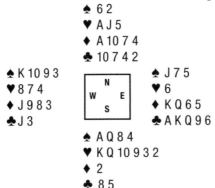

```
                        ♠ 6 2
                        ♥ A J 5
                        ♦ A 10 7 4
                        ♣ 10 7 4 2
        ♠ K 10 9 3                      ♠ J 7 5
        ♥ 8 7 4         ┌─────────┐     ♥ 6
        ♦ J 9 8 3       │    N    │     ♦ K Q 6 5
        ♣ J 3           │ W     E │     ♣ A K Q 9 6
                        │    S    │
                        └─────────┘
                        ♠ A Q 8 4
                        ♥ K Q 10 9 3 2
                        ♦ 2
                        ♣ 8 5
```

You reach game in hearts after East has opened 1♣. West leads the jack of clubs and continues with another club. East wins with the queen and plays the ace of clubs. What is your plan to make the contract?

You begin by counting the losers in the long-trump hand. You have three potential losers in spades, none in trumps and none in diamonds. In clubs you started with two losers and the defenders have already taken their two tricks. So, you need to reduce three spade losers to one. You can finesse the queen on the first round. If this loses, you will need to ruff your remaining two spades in dummy. How should the play go?

You ruff the third club high, to prevent an overruff, and must now take a spade finesse. How will you cross to dummy? Suppose you play a trump to the ace. When the spade finesse loses, an alert West will play another trump. You will not then be able to ruff both your remaining spade losers. Instead you should cross to dummy with the ♦A. You can then ruff two spades, even if West returns a trump when the spade finesse loses.

Summary

✓ To plan a suit contract you should count the potential losers in the long-trump hand. You then seek the safest way to reduce the total to the required number. (For example, if you can see five possible losers in a major-suit game, you must dispose of two of the losers.)

✓ You can dispose of losers in three main ways:
  • ruffing a loser in the dummy
  • taking a finesse
  • discarding a loser on surplus winners in the dummy.

HOW TO PLAN A SUIT CONTRACT

NOW TRY THESE...

1)

♠ Q J 3
♥ 8 3
♦ A Q 6 4
♣ A 10 7 4

♠ A K 10 7 4 2
♥ A 10 5 4
♦ K 2
♣ 3

West leads the ♣K against your small slam in spades. Plan the play.

2)

♠ A 3
♥ 10 6 2
♦ 10 9 6 4 3
♣ Q J 7

♠ K Q J 10 6 4
♥ A 7 3
♦ A Q
♣ K 2

You reach four spades and West leads the ♥K. Plan the play.

3)

♠ K 3
♥ 9 8 5
♦ A K 7 6 2
♣ 8 6 3

♠ A Q J 10 6 2
♥ —
♦ 8 5 3
♣ A K J 10

West leads the ♥Q against your small slam in spades. Plan the play.

ANSWERS

1) Your only possible losers are in hearts. To reduce the three losers to one, you should plan to ruff one heart and discard another on the diamonds. Suppose you start by drawing two rounds of trumps and find that they break 3-1. When you subsequently duck a heart, to prepare for a heart ruff, the defenders may draw dummy's last trump, depriving you of your ruff. To avoid this fate, you should draw just one round of trumps, with the ace, and then play ace and another heart. When you regain the lead you will ruff a heart with the jack and draw trumps. You can then play three rounds of diamonds, discarding your last heart loser.

2) You have two potential losers in hearts, one in diamonds and one in clubs. There is little you can do about the heart losers, once the suit has been led. Nor can you avoid losing a trick to the ace of clubs. In diamonds you could take a successful finesse. That would be only a 50% chance, though. What else can you try? A better idea is to set up a discard on the club suit. Suppose you draw trumps first and then lead the king of clubs. A skilled defender will hold up the ace of clubs for one round, to cut you off from the dummy. To prevent this defense, lead the ♣K at Trick 2. If the defenders hold up the ace, play another club. The defenders will win and cash two hearts. When you regain the lead, draw two rounds of trumps with the king and ace. You can then play a club winner, discarding the queen of diamonds. Finally, you return to your hand to draw the outstanding trumps.

3) Viewing the situation from the long-trump hand, you have no potential losers in the major suits. There is one possible loser in diamonds and another in clubs. You cannot avoid the diamond loser. A repeated finesse in clubs might rescue you in that suit. Before relying on this, you should aim to set up the diamond suit, to provide two discards. Ruff the heart lead and draw trumps. Your next move is to duck a round of diamonds, aiming to set up the suit if it is divided 3-2. Win the return and test the diamond suit. If it does break 3-2, you can discard the jack and ten of clubs on the fourth and fifth rounds of diamonds. If diamonds break 4-1, no discards will be available. You will need to find East with the ♣Q. You can use the ace and king of diamonds as entries for the club finesses.

FINESSING INTO THE SAFE HAND

When you are able to finesse a suit in either hand, the consideration of which of your opponents you want to prevent from getting the lead is often most important.
W. Dalton. *Practical Bridge. 1908*

Whether you are playing in a suit contract or in notrump, you will often reach a situation where one defender is **dangerous** and the other is **safe**. A defender may be dangerous because he has tricks to cash. He may be dangerous because he can lead through an unprotected king. In such situations your finessing strategy will be aimed at keeping the 'danger hand', as it is called, off lead. Look at this deal:

```
              ♠ 7 3
              ♥ Q 5
              ♦ A J 10 9 4 2
              ♣ J 10 5
♠ A 10 8 6 2   ┌─────────┐   ♠ J 9 4
♥ 9 8 3        │    N    │   ♥ 10 7 4 2
♦ 7 6          │  W   E  │   ♦ K 8 5
♣ K 7 3        │    S    │   ♣ 8 6 2
              └─────────┘
              ♠ K Q 5
              ♥ A K J 6
              ♦ Q 3
              ♣ A Q 9 4
```

West	North	East	South
			2NT
pass	3NT	all pass	

BY THE WAY

Look back at the spade situation in this 3NT contract:

```
        ♠ 7 3
♠ A 10 8 6 2  ┌───┐  ♠ J 9 4
        │ N │
        │W E│
        │ S │
        └───┘
        ♠ K Q 5
```

West leads the six to East's jack. Does it make any difference whether you win with the king or the queen? It sure does! If you win with the queen, West will know that you also hold the king (because otherwise East would have played the king). If instead you win with the king, West will have no idea who holds the queen. When he gains the lead he may be tempted to play another spade in the hope that East holds the card. As declarer, it is nearly always right to win with the higher of two touching cards.

West leads the ♠6 against your contract of 3NT and you win East's jack. What next? You have potential finesses in diamonds and in clubs. Which one should you take?

Suppose your eye is attracted to the longer diamond suit. You run the ♦Q and East wins with the king. Retribution will be swift. East will lead a spade through your remaining honor and you will go down. East is the danger hand because he is the defender who will be able to lead through your remaining spade holding. Finessing 'into the danger hand' is something you should try to avoid. If the finesse loses, you will be in big trouble.

Suppose instead that you cross to the ♥Q and take the club finesse, running the jack. That loses too, as the cards lie, but you will still make the contract! You are finessing 'into the safe hand'. West cannot play spades profitably from his side of the table. (He will give you a second spade trick if he does.) If he returns any other suit, you will make nine tricks: one spade, four hearts, one diamond and three clubs.

Finessing in diamonds risks the contract. Finessing in clubs guarantees the contract. Not a difficult choice, is it?

The same principle applies when you have a two-way finesse in a suit.

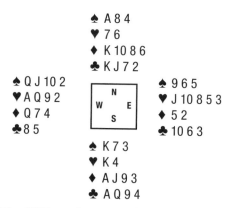

After a 1NT - 3NT auction, West leads the ♠Q. How will you play safely to make the contract?

You have eight top tricks and must seek a ninth. How about leading towards the ♥K? Only a thrill seeker would play the contract that way. If West held the heart ace, the defenders could take at least five heart tricks. Suppose instead that you cash the ace of diamonds and run the diamond jack. You have a 50% chance of the diamond finesse working. The finesse is into the danger hand, though — into the hand that can lead a heart through your king. If the diamond finesse loses and West has the ♥A, there is every chance that you will go down.

You have a two-way finesse in diamonds. You can finesse either defender for the missing queen. Since you need only three diamond tricks to make the contract, you don't have to guess correctly in the suit. You can guarantee the contract by playing a diamond to the king and then running the ♦10 into the safe West hand. The finesse will lose, when the cards lie as in our diagram, but you will still make the contract. You had eight top tricks at the start and a third trick from the diamond suit will bring the total to nine.

On the next deal you have a choice between a straightforward finesse and a ruffing finesse. Which would you have chosen?

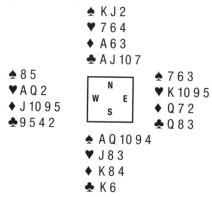

West leads the ♦J against your game in spades. You can count three losers in the heart suit and a further loser in diamonds. One of these can be discarded on the surplus winner in clubs, but how should you play the clubs? You have a choice of finesses in the suit. You can cash the king and play a low card to the jack, hoping that West holds the club queen. If that finesse loses, however, the defenders will be able to score three heart tricks, defeating the game.

A better idea is to take a ruffing finesse. Win the diamond lead with the king and draw trumps in three rounds. You then play the king and ace of clubs and lead the club jack. When the queen appears from East, you ruff in your hand and cross to the ♦A (which is why you won the diamond lead with the king!). You can then play the established ♣10, throwing a heart loser. Ten tricks are now yours.

Even if West held the ♣Q, this line of play would still work. You would throw one heart on the ♣J and the defenders would score just a club and two hearts. When you regained the lead you would throw the diamond loser on the established ♣10.

Summary

✓ When you have a choice of finesses to take, choose the one that will be 'into the safe hand'. Even if it loses, the defender will not be able to do any damage.

✓ When you have a two-way finesse to take, and don't mind losing one trick in the suit, take the finesse 'into the safe hand'.

✓ Occasionally you will have a choice between a normal finesse and a ruffing finesse (with A-Q-J-x opposite a singleton, for example). Choose the finesse that will leave you with a chance of making the contract even if it fails.

FINESSING INTO THE SAFE HAND

NOW TRY THESE...

1)

♠ Q 4
♥ A 7 2
♦ A 3 2
♣ K J 9 6 2

♠ K 7 5
♥ K Q 9
♦ J 10 6 4
♣ A 10 5

West leads the ♠6 against 3NT and dummy's ♠Q wins. How will you play?

2)

♠ 7 5
♥ A Q 3
♦ A Q J 10 6
♣ J 7 6

♠ A 9 4
♥ J 7
♦ K 8 3
♣ A Q 10 8 3

West leads the ♠3 against 3NT. East wins with the king and returns the ♠10. How will you play the contract?

3)

♠ A J 8 4
♥ 8 2
♦ K Q J 7
♣ 7 6 4

♠ K 10 9 3
♥ A K 5
♦ A 8 6
♣ K 8 3

West leads the ♥Q against your spade game. How will you play?

ANSWERS

1) After the spade queen wins, you have seven top tricks. The club suit will provide two extra tricks, even if a finesse loses. East is the danger hand because he can lead through your remaining ♠K-7. You should therefore finesse clubs into the safe (West) hand. Lead the ♣J at Trick 2, letting it ride unless East covers with the queen. If West wins with the queen he can do you no damage. You will win the return and make the contract. If instead the ♣J wins the trick, continue with a low club to the ten.

   Note that it would not be a good idea to cash the ♣K before finessing the ten. You would not then be able to pick up Q-x-x-x in the East hand. To set up a fourth club trick you would have to allow East on lead with the ♣Q. Defeat would surely follow.

2) It looks as if spades are 5-3. Why is that? Because East returned the ♠10. If he held four spades he would have returned the ♠2. You should hold up the ace of spades until the third round, exhausting East of the suit. You can count eight top tricks and it is perhaps tempting to take a club finesse, netting several overtricks if the finesse wins. This finesse is into the dangerous hand, however. If it loses, West will cash his spades to defeat the contract. A better idea is to run the ♥J, since this finesse is into the safe hand. If it loses, East will have no spade to return (unless spades started 4-4 and the suit poses no threat). Dummy's ♥Q will then be established as a ninth trick. Remember: when you have a choice of finesses, you should finesse into the safe hand.

3) You win the heart lead and turn your mind towards drawing trumps. You can finesse either defender for the trump queen. East is the danger hand because he could switch to a club through your king, putting the contract at risk. You should therefore take the trump finesse into the safe (West) hand. Even if it loses, West will not be able to damage you. Eventually you will ruff a heart in dummy, draw any trumps that remain and throw one of your club losers on dummy's fourth diamond.

PLAYING A CROSSRUFF

 Study the two hands carefully, see where they will combine to your advantage. **W. Dalton.** *Practical Bridge. 1908*

We have already seen that taking a ruff in the short-trump hand gives you an extra trick, whereas ruffing in the long-trump hand does not. Sometimes it is not practical to take ruffs in one hand and then draw trumps in the other. Instead you have to take ruffs in both hands, making each of your trumps separately. The play is known as a **crossruff**.

One of the most common scenarios for a crossruff occurs when your trumps are weak in both hands. Look at this example:

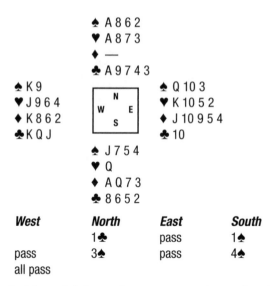

	♠ A 8 6 2		
	♥ A 8 7 3		
	♦ —		
	♣ A 9 7 4 3		

West	North	East	South
	1♣	pass	1♠
pass	3♠	pass	4♠
all pass			

West leads the king of clubs against your game in spades. Looking at the diagram, you may think that you are destined to lose two clubs and two trump tricks. There's a chance to make several tricks by ruffing hearts and diamonds, though. If you can make six small trumps by ruffing the red suits, your four aces will bring the total to ten!

You win the club lead, play the ace of hearts and ruff a heart. After cashing the ace of diamonds, you ruff alternately in diamonds and hearts. The defenders have to follow all the way, you are pleased to see. You soon have nine tricks before you and dummy's ace of trumps will make it ten.

On the next deal your trumps are stronger but you do not have the entries to take several ruffs in one hand before drawing trumps in the other. Once again, the answer is a crossruff.

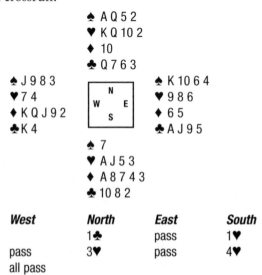

West	North	East	South
	1♣	pass	1♥
pass	3♥	pass	4♥
all pass			

West leads the ♦K against your game in hearts. How should you play the contract?

Suppose you fail to make a plan and draw trumps straight away. Where will ten tricks come from then? You are woefully short of high cards and will fall well short of your target. A better idea is to aim to score your two aces along with eight trump tricks. To achieve this you must score all eight of your trumps separately, by taking ruffs in both hands.

You win the diamond lead with the ace and ruff a diamond immediately. You take this first ruff with dummy's low trump, leaving the high trumps for later — when there will be more risk of an overruff. You cash dummy's ♠A and ruff a spade in the South hand, again using a low trump. When you ruff a second diamond in the dummy, East shows out. Since this ruff is with a high trump, East cannot overruff. You ruff a spade with the last low trump in the South hand and the contract is guaranteed when this passes by safely. A diamond ruff, a spade ruff and a fourth diamond ruff — all with high trumps — bring your total to nine tricks. Since the ace of trumps is still in your hand, you make the game exactly.

What was the main point to remember about that deal? *You took the early ruffs with low trumps, saving the high trumps for the later ruffs.*

The next deal illustrates a second important point to remember when you tackle a crossruff. Let's take a look at it.

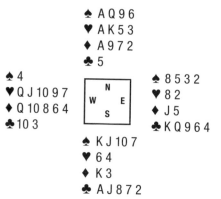

```
              ♠ A Q 9 6
              ♥ A K 5 3
              ♦ A 9 7 2
              ♣ 5
    ♠ 4                      ♠ 8 5 3 2
    ♥ Q J 10 9 7     N       ♥ 8 2
    ♦ Q 10 8 6 4   W   E     ♦ J 5
    ♣ 10 3           S       ♣ K Q 9 6 4
              ♠ K J 10 7
              ♥ 6 4
              ♦ K 3
              ♣ A J 8 7 2
```

West leads the ♥Q against your ambitious grand slam in spades. How would you play the contract?

You have five winners in the side suits. If you can make all eight trumps separately, this will bring your total to thirteen tricks. There should be no problem in doing this. You can ruff four clubs in the dummy, two hearts and two diamonds in the South hand.

Suppose you win the heart lead with the ace, cash the king of hearts successfully and play a third heart. Disaster! East will discard a diamond. When you eventually try to cash the two top diamonds, East will ruff the second round and you will go down.

BY THE WAY

The term 'side suit' refers to the three suits that are not trumps. To 'cash all the winners in the side suits' means to play all the top cards outside the trump suit.

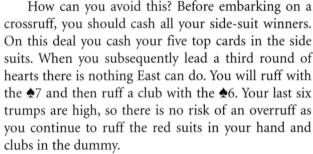

How can you avoid this? Before embarking on a crossruff, you should cash all your side-suit winners. On this deal you cash your five top cards in the side suits. When you subsequently lead a third round of hearts there is nothing East can do. You will ruff with the ♠7 and then ruff a club with the ♠6. Your last six trumps are high, so there is no risk of an overruff as you continue to ruff the red suits in your hand and clubs in the dummy.

Perhaps you noticed that on the last two deals, a trump lead would have worked well for the defenders. It would have prevented you from scoring all your trumps separately. Diagnosing when it is right to lead a trump is not at all easy — even for experts!

Summary

✓ When you have few high-card winners but a side-suit shortage in both hands, consider a crossruff. You plan to score all your trumps separately.

✓ On most crossruff deals you take the early ruffs with low trumps, saving the high trumps for later, when there is more risk of an overruff.

✓ Before embarking on a crossruff, cash the side-suit winners in both hands. If you fail to do this, the defenders may take discards while you are crossruffing and eventually be in a position to ruff your winners.

PLAYING A CROSSRUFF

1)

♠ Q J 9 8
♥ 9 7 2
♦ A K 10 4 2
♣ 8

```
    N
  W   E
    S
```

♠ A K 10 3
♥ A 8 5
♦ 6
♣ A K 10 5 3

West leads the ♥K against six spades. Plan the play.

2)

♠ Q J 9 5
♥ 9 6 5 3
♦ A 10 4 2
♣ 8

```
    N
  W   E
    S
```

♠ A K 8 3
♥ A 8 2
♦ 6 3
♣ A J 5 3

West leads the ♥K against four spades. Plan the play.

3)

♠ A Q 10 2
♥ A J 9 7 2
♦ A K 7
♣ J

```
    N
  W   E
    S
```

♠ K J 9 3
♥ 5
♦ Q 10 4
♣ A 8 7 3 2

West leads the ♣K against your grand slam (yes!) in spades. Plan the play.

ANSWERS

1) You have five top tricks in the side suits, so seven trump tricks made on a crossruff will bring the total to twelve. Win the heart lead and cash the top cards in the minors. You now ruff three clubs in dummy and three diamonds in your hand. The main point of the deal is that you should not risk a diamond ruff with the ♠3 (West might overruff). Take all three diamond ruffs with high trumps. Five side-suit winners plus six high ruffs will bring your total to eleven. A master trump will remain in dummy to take the twelfth trick.

2) You have only three side-suit winners and must aim for seven trump tricks to bring the total to ten. Win the heart lead and play ace and another diamond, preparing to ruff some diamonds in the South hand. When they have taken their two heart winners the defenders may play a round of trumps (somewhat late — a trump lead would have beaten you!). After winning the trump switch, you must take three club ruffs and two diamond ruffs. So, play the ace of clubs first. Club ruff, diamond ruff, club ruff, diamond ruff, club ruff. You have nine tricks before you and the master trump in your hand will make the total ten. You take the early ruffs with low trumps, and where necessary, the later ruffs with high trumps.

3) Once again you are lucky to have avoided a trump lead. Five winners in the side suits, along with eight trump tricks (four ruffs in each hand), will bring the total to thirteen. Is there anything important to remember before you start the crossruff? Yes, you must cash all the side-suit winners. That means steeling yourself to play three rounds of diamonds, even though trumps have not been drawn. When this passes by successfully, you play the ace of hearts and take the first two ruffs with low trumps. 'I make the rest of the tricks on a high crossruff,' you say impressively as you table your remaining cards. Grand slam made!

CHAPTER 12

CREATING EXTRA ENTRIES

Managing the entries to both hands is one of the most important aspects of playing the dummy. In this chapter we will see how you can create extra entries to the weaker hand.

First, let's see how you can manipulate a single suit to give you an extra entry. Suppose you are blessed with this club suit:

♣ A 7 3 2

♣ 9 6   ♣ 10 8 5

♣ K Q J 4

If you play the suit in normal fashion, cashing the three honors in the South hand and then leading the ♣4 to the ace, this will give you only one entry to the dummy. Suppose instead that you start with the king and queen, discovering that the suit breaks 3-2. You can then overtake the jack with the ace on the third round. After making use of this entry, by leading some other suit from dummy, you can overtake the ♣4 with the ♣7. This will give you a second entry to dummy.

Here is a similar position:

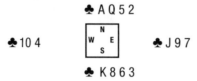

♣ A Q 5 2

♣ 10 4   ♣ J 9 7

♣ K 8 6 3

The king wins the first round. You lead the eight to the ace next, followed later by the six to the queen. You will then have an extra entry to dummy on the fourth round — you can lead the three to the five.

Let's see a whole deal where you can make use of this technique:

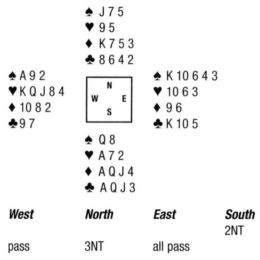

♠ J 7 5
♥ 9 5
♦ K 7 5 3
♣ 8 6 4 2

♠ A 9 2   ♠ K 10 6 4 3
♥ K Q J 8 4   ♥ 10 6 3
♦ 10 8 2   ♦ 9 6
♣ 9 7   ♣ K 10 5

♠ Q 8
♥ A 7 2
♦ A Q J 4
♣ A Q J 3

West	North	East	South
			2NT
pass	3NT	all pass	

West leads the ♥K. You have six top tricks and will need three more tricks from the club suit. Since you are not afraid of any switch, you might as well hold up the ♥A until the third round and discard a club from dummy. What next?

Suppose you lead the ♦4 to dummy's king and take one club finesse. Since you have no further entry to dummy, you will have to play the ace of clubs next and hope that East started with only a doubleton king in the suit. That's asking rather a lot. How can you do better?

You must manipulate the diamond suit to give yourself a second entry to dummy. You begin by cashing the ace and queen of diamonds, confirming that the suit breaks 3-2. You can then afford to overtake the jack of diamonds with the king on the third round. A finesse of the club queen succeeds and you re-enter dummy by overtaking the ♦4 with the ♦7. When you repeat the club finesse West follows suit. That's good news. You play the ace of clubs, dropping East's king, and you now have nine tricks.

What would have happened if diamonds had broken 4-1? You could not then overtake the jack on the third round, without allowing the defenders to win the fourth round. With only one entry to dummy, you would have had to hope that East had started with a doubleton king of clubs.

Sometimes you have to risk an otherwise unnecessary finesse in order to seek a vital extra entry. On the next deal you need to set up dummy's diamond suit and dummy is short of entries.

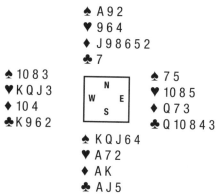

```
              ♠ A 9 2
              ♥ 9 6 4
              ♦ J 9 8 6 5 2
              ♣ 7
  ♠ 10 8 3                   ♠ 7 5
  ♥ K Q J 3        N         ♥ 10 8 5
  ♦ 10 4      W        E     ♦ Q 7 3
  ♣ K 9 6 2        S         ♣ Q 10 8 4 3
              ♠ K Q J 6 4
              ♥ A 7 2
              ♦ A K
              ♣ A J 5
```

You reach an adventurous small slam in spades and West leads the ♥K. How can you make twelve tricks?

It is no good ruffing two clubs in dummy. That would still leave you with two heart losers. To make the slam you must set up dummy's diamonds and then reach the established cards in the suit. After winning the heart lead with the ace, you cash the ace and king of diamonds. If the sun is shining and the diamond queen falls doubleton, you will draw trumps in three rounds, ending in the dummy, and make all thirteen tricks. When the cards lie as in the diagram, both defenders follow to the diamonds but the queen does not fall. You now need two entries to the dummy — one to ruff a diamond in order to set up the suit, another to reach the established diamonds. The ace of trumps will provide one entry. What is the best chance of a second?

After drawing one round of trumps with the king, you should finesse dummy's nine of trumps. (This is a better chance than rising with the ace, hoping that East started with ♠10-x and that the ten will fall.) When the finesse succeeds, you breathe a sigh of relief and ruff a diamond with the queen. You then cross to dummy's ace of trumps and play the remaining diamonds. Away go three of your four losers and you make the small slam.

Another way to create an extra entry is by overtaking a singleton honor with a higher honor. It is necessary on this deal:

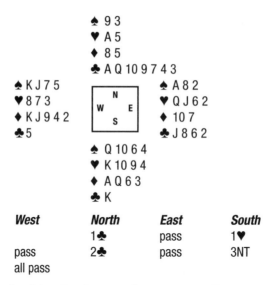

♠ 9 3
♥ A 5
♦ 8 5
♣ A Q 10 9 7 4 3

♠ K J 7 5
♥ 8 7 3
♦ K J 9 4 2
♣ 5

♠ A 8 2
♥ Q J 6 2
♦ 10 7
♣ J 8 6 2

♠ Q 10 6 4
♥ K 10 9 4
♦ A Q 6 3
♣ K

West	North	East	South
	1♣	pass	1♥
pass	2♣	pass	3NT
all pass			

West leads the ♦4 to East's ten and your queen. Suppose you give the matter little thought and cash the king of clubs, continuing with a heart to the ace. When you play the ace of clubs West will show out and there will be no way to recover.

Since you do not need all seven club tricks to make your game, you should overtake the king of clubs with the ace at Trick 2. This gives you a second entry to dummy. You can then cash the club queen and force out East's jack of clubs, making the game easily.

Summary

✔ By unblocking high cards under higher cards in the dummy, you can set up extra entries. With A-Q-10-8 in dummy and K-J-9-3 in hand, for example, you could overtake king, jack, nine and three to create four entries!

✔ Sometimes you have to risk an otherwise unnecessary finesse in order to create a vital extra entry.

CREATING EXTRA ENTRIES

NOW TRY THESE...

1)

♠ 8 5 3
♥ 10 7 4
♦ 7 6 2
♣ A K 5 2

```
      N
  W       E
      S
```

♠ A Q
♥ K Q 5
♦ A Q J 10
♣ 9 8 6 4

Playing in 3NT, you win West's ♠J lead with the queen. What next?

2)

♠ A 10 9 8 3
♥ 7 5
♦ 8 5 2
♣ K 7 4

```
      N
  W       E
      S
```

♠ K Q
♥ A K 8 4
♦ A 9 6 3
♣ A 5 2

West leads the ♣6 against 3NT. How will you play the contract?

3)

♠ Q 10 4
♥ 10 6 2
♦ 8 7 3
♣ 9 7 6 2

```
      N
  W       E
      S
```

♠ K 6 5
♥ A J 3
♦ A K 5
♣ A Q J 3

Against 3NT, West leads the ♠3 to dummy's ♠4 and East's ace. How will you plan the play?

ANSWERS

1) Two spade tricks, four diamonds and three clubs will bring your total to nine. If East holds K-x-x-x in diamonds, you will need to take three finesses in the suit. That will require three entries to dummy in the club suit. Lead the nine of clubs to the ace at Trick 2 and play a diamond to the queen. If the finesse wins, lead the eight of clubs to the king and play a diamond to the jack. Now lead the six of clubs, playing dummy's two. The defenders will win and doubtless clear the spade suit (playing a heart is no better for them). Feeling pleased with yourself, you can now lead the four of clubs to dummy's five, reaching dummy for the third time. A diamond to the ten will give you a total of four diamond tricks, even if East started with K-x-x-x in the suit. Impressive, yes?

2) You can count five top tricks outside the spade suit, so you need only four spade tricks to bring your total to nine. Win the club lead immediately, with the ace. To protect yourself against a 4-2 spade break, the best play in that suit is to cash the king and overtake the queen with the ace on the second round, to gain an entry. Knocking out the spade jack will then set up the suit, however the defenders' cards divide. You will need to reach dummy to play the established winners in spades, and the only available entry is the king of clubs. That's why you needed to win the opening club lead with your ace!

3) West's ♠3 lead and East's play of the ♠A both suggest that West has led from the spade jack. When East wins the first trick with the ace, you should follow with the king! You will then have two small spades facing dummy's Q-10 and a finesse in the suit will give you two entries to dummy. If East switches to a diamond at Trick 2, win with the ace and finesse the ♠10. You can then finesse the club queen, return to dummy with the spade queen and finesse again in clubs, hoping to score four tricks in the suit.

    If you are unlucky and the club finesse loses, you will have to use dummy's remaining spade entry to lead a heart to the jack. You may then recover if East holds both the king and queen of hearts.

AVOIDING A RUFF

 The declarer has much in his favor, owing to his power of combining the strength of his two hands, while his opponents are scrapping about to find out what each other holds.
W. Dalton. *Practical Bridge. 1908*

A defender leads a side-suit singleton, his partner winning with the ace and giving him a ruff. Unpleasant, yes, but there was nothing you could do about it. In this chapter we will look at some happier situations where, as declarer, you *can* prevent an adverse ruff.

Sometimes all that is needed is to vary the way you would normally play the trump suit. Look at this deal:

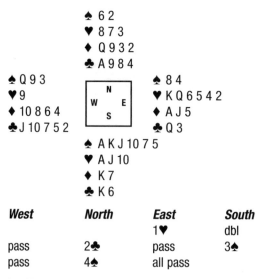

♠ 6 2
♥ 8 7 3
♦ Q 9 3 2
♣ A 9 8 4

♠ Q 9 3   ♠ 8 4
♥ 9   ♥ K Q 6 5 4 2
♦ 10 8 6 4   ♦ A J 5
♣ J 10 7 5 2   ♣ Q 3

♠ A K J 10 7 5
♥ A J 10
♦ K 7
♣ K 6

West	North	East	South
		1♥	dbl
pass	2♣	pass	3♠
pass	4♠	all pass	

West leads the ♥9 against your game in spades and you win East's queen with the ace. What now?

Missing five trumps to the queen, you would normally take a finesse in the suit. Let's see what happens if you do that. You first play the ace of trumps then cross to the ace of clubs to finesse the jack of trumps. West wins with the queen and reaches his partner's hand with a diamond to the ace. The queen of hearts is the defenders' third trick and a heart ruff puts the game down one.

It was entirely predictable that you might suffer a heart ruff, even if West's opening lead was from a doubleton. To avoid losing two trump tricks (the queen as well as a ruff), you should play the ace and king of trumps. The queen does not fall, as it happens, but you will lose only one trump trick and make the contract.

This is an example of what is known as a 'safety play'. You give up the best chance of an overtrick (finessing East for Q-x-x in the trump suit), but in exchange you maximize your chance of making the contract.

Another way to prevent a ruff is to break the communication between the defenders.

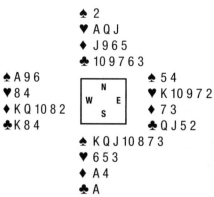

♠ 2
♥ A Q J
♦ J 9 6 5
♣ 10 9 7 6 3

♠ A 9 6   ♠ 5 4
♥ 8 4   ♥ K 10 9 7 2
♦ K Q 10 8 2   ♦ 7 3
♣ K 8 4   ♣ Q J 5 2

♠ K Q J 10 8 7 3
♥ 6 5 3
♦ A 4
♣ A

West	North	East	South
1♦	pass	1♥	4♠
all pass			

West leads the ♥8 against your game in spades. If this is a singleton, you will do best to rise with dummy's ace. (East will then have no entry to deliver a heart ruff.) However, it is more likely that the lead is a doubleton. Let's see what happens in that case, if you win the first trick.

When you play trumps, West will win with the ace and cross to partner's hand with a second round of hearts. He will ruff the next round of hearts, giving the defenders three tricks, and an eventual diamond trick will put you down one.

To prevent this, you should play dummy's queen of hearts on the first trick. East wins with the king and the contract is now safe. You will win the return and play trumps. When West takes his ace of trumps he will have no route to the East hand. You will lose just one spade, one heart and a diamond.

One of the most spectacular plays in bridge is aimed at preventing an adverse ruff by cutting the defenders' communications.

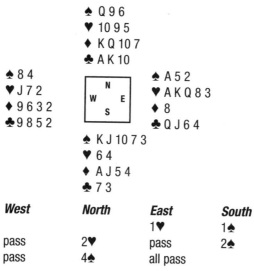

```
                    ♠ Q 9 6
                    ♥ 10 9 5
                    ♦ K Q 10 7
                    ♣ A K 10
    ♠ 8 4                        ♠ A 5 2
    ♥ J 7 2          N           ♥ A K Q 8 3
    ♦ 9 6 3 2      W   E         ♦ 8
    ♣ 9 8 5 2        S           ♣ Q J 6 4
                    ♠ K J 10 7 3
                    ♥ 6 4
                    ♦ A J 5 4
                    ♣ 7 3
```

West	North	East	South
		1♥	1♠
pass	2♥	pass	2♠
pass	4♠	all pass	

You make a somewhat light overcall and partner allows you no leeway, carrying on to game. West leads the ♥2 and East wins with the queen. How will you react when East switches unexpectedly to the ♦8?

If East held a doubleton diamond, it would not be very attractive for him to switch into a K-Q-10 combination. No, his line of defense strongly suggests that he holds only one diamond. What will happen if you simply win the diamond switch and play a trump? East will win with the ace and play a low heart to West's jack, underleading his ace-king. A diamond ruff will then beat the contract. How can you prevent this?

There is only one hope. You must play the ace and king of clubs, followed by the ten. If East wins this trick, as you must hope, you will throw away your remaining heart. Do you see the effect of this? You have not reduced the number of losers directly, because you have lost a club trick instead of a heart trick. What you have done is to cut the link between the defenders' hands. Since East now has no way to reach the West hand he cannot receive a diamond ruff. When you regain the lead you will play trumps and eventually lose just one trump, one heart and one club. The technique is picturesquely known as the **Scissors Coup**, because you cut the defenders' communications. It is an example of a **loser-on-loser play**: you exchange one loser for another, meanwhile gaining a tactical advantage.

BY THE WAY

Suppose East's clubs were Q-9-6-4 instead of Q-J-6-4. He could then beat you by playing low when you led the ♣10 on the third round. If you discarded your last heart, West would win with the ♣J and give partner a diamond ruff. If instead East's clubs were Q-9-4, he could beat you by unblocking the queen under the ace or king. Again his partner would be able to win the third round of clubs with the jack.

Summary

✓ When you suspect an adverse ruff, be wary of taking a trump finesse. If the finesse fails, the defenders may take a ruff and you will then lose two trump tricks. Play trumps from the top instead and you may restrict your trumps losers to one.

✓ Holding up an ace is a familiar technique in notrump. It can prove valuable in a suit contract too. If one defender has a doubleton, you may cut communications that the defenders would otherwise use to obtain a ruff or to cash winners.

✓ Sometimes you hold a singleton in a suit that the defenders may use as communications for a ruff. To break the link between the defenders you may be able to make a **loser-on-loser play**, discarding your singleton on a losing card in another suit. When the safe defender has to win the trick you avoid the ruff.

AVOIDING A RUFF

1)

     ♠ 9 4
     ♥ A J 2
     ♦ J 9 7 4 2
     ♣ A K J

     ♠ K Q J 10 8 7 3
     ♥ 8 6 5
     ♦ 6
     ♣ 5 3

West opened the bidding with a weak 2♥, showing six hearts and 5-9 points. He subsequently leads the ♥K against four spades. Plan the play.

2)

     ♠ J 9 5 4
     ♥ Q 10 8 4
     ♦ 10 2
     ♣ K 10 7

     N
   W E
     S

     ♠ A Q 10 8 3
     ♥ A K J 5
     ♦ 6 3
     ♣ A 5

West leads the ♥2 against four spades. Plan the play.

3)

     ♠ A 7 5 2
     ♥ Q 9 4 3
     ♦ A 10 7
     ♣ A 5

     N
   W E
     S

     ♠ Q 10 9 3
     ♥ A K J 10 5
     ♦ 4
     ♣ K Q 7

West leads the ♣8 against your small slam in hearts. Plan the play.

AVOIDING A RUFF

ANSWERS

1) Win the heart lead immediately, since a duck will almost certainly result in a ruff at Trick 2. (West opened 2♥, remember, showing a six-card suit.) If West holds the ace of trumps, it is unlikely that you can avoid a heart ruff. If East has that card, and you play a trump at Trick 2, he will win with the ace and may be able to cross to partner's hand in diamonds. West will then cash the queen of hearts and give East a ruff, beating the contract.

   Instead, you should play the ace, king and jack of clubs. If East covers the jack of clubs with the queen, throw your singleton diamond to cut the link to the West hand. If instead East plays low on the third round of clubs, it is reasonable to place the club queen with West. Your best chance is to ruff and play a trump. You will still make the contract if East holds all three top diamonds (which is quite likely when West has already shown up with the ♥K-Q and the ♣Q). East will not then be able to reach partner's hand when he wins the trump ace.

2) Since you hold all the heart honors, either in your own hand or the dummy, West's ♥2 lead is likely to be a singleton. Suppose you win in the dummy and take a losing trump finesse. West may win with the king and cross to the East hand with a diamond. A heart ruff, followed by a second loser in diamonds, will then beat the contract. A better idea is to play ace and another trump, which will save you a ruff when West holds a doubleton king in the trump suit. (If West has K-x-x in the trump suit, there is nothing you can do.) You don't mind losing a trump trick, provided you don't lose a ruff too. You can afford two diamond losers and one trump loser.

3) West's ♠8 opening lead is likely to be either a doubleton or a singleton. If you play low from dummy at Trick 1 and the lead is a singleton, East will win with the king and give his partner a spade ruff. Not the best of starts in a slam! Instead you should win with dummy's ace of spades and draw trumps. You can then lead a low spade from dummy and finesse the ten, if East plays low.

   (If you're worried that West may have made a fancy lead from J-8-4, K-8-4 or K-J-8-4 don't be! This kind of lead is very rare. It is much more likely that West has led a singleton.)

CHOOSING WHICH SUIT TO PLAY

 Go at once for the suit you have the best chance of establishing in either hand. **W. Dalton.** *Practical Bridge. 1908*

In the chapters on 'planning a notrump contract' and 'finessing into the safe hand', we have already touched on the subject of choosing which suit to play first. It is such an important subject, indeed at the very heart of notrump play, that we will look at it one more time in this chapter.

Hands like the next one are dealt on countless occasions.

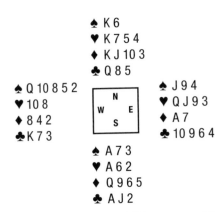

```
              ♠ K 6
              ♥ K 7 5 4
              ♦ K J 10 3
              ♣ Q 8 5
♠ Q 10 8 5 2       ┌─────┐        ♠ J 9 4
♥ 10 8             │  N  │        ♥ Q J 9 3
♦ 8 4 2          W │ ♦ E │ E      ♦ A 7
♣ K 7 3            │  S  │        ♣ 10 9 6 4
                   └─────┘
              ♠ A 7 3
              ♥ A 6 2
              ♦ Q 9 6 5
              ♣ A J 2
```

West leads the ♠5 against your 3NT contract. How would you plan the play?

Many players would go down without even realizing that they had done anything wrong. After winning the first or second round of spades they would attack diamonds, their longest suit. East would win with the ace and clear the spade suit. When the club finesse lost, West would beat the contract by cashing his spade winners. (Playing hearts would be no better for declarer.)

What went wrong? Declarer had two potential stoppers to knock out, the king of clubs and the ace of diamonds. In such a situation you must 'attack the entry to the danger hand'. In other words, you must knock out first the stopper held by the danger hand — usually the player who has the greater length in the suit that was led. On the present deal you have no idea who holds the ♦A. What you do know is that when you play a club to the jack only West can gain the lead. After ducking the first spade and winning the second round with dummy's king, you should play a club to the jack. Suppose first that the finesse wins. You will then have six top tricks and can set up the diamonds to establish three more.

BY THE WAY

Look back to the full diagram and imagine that you hold the king of clubs instead of the ace. You would then have two aces to knock out. Again you could make the contract if you knocked out West's ace first. Of course, it would be a complete guess whether West held the club ace or the diamond ace. On the original deal no guess was involved.

What if the club finesse loses? You will have knocked out the entry to the danger hand. West will no doubt play a third round of spades to your ace but you will still make the contract if East holds the diamond ace. (If West holds both the ♣K and the ♦A you were doomed anyway.)

Let's look, for the first time, at a 3NT contract where you have what might be called two and a half stoppers (A-K-10 in the suit led).

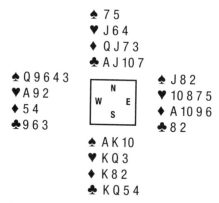

```
              ♠ 7 5
              ♥ J 6 4
              ♦ Q J 7 3
              ♣ A J 10 7
♠ Q 9 6 4 3        N        ♠ J 8 2
♥ A 9 2        W       E    ♥ 10 8 7 5
♦ 5 4              S        ♦ A 10 9 6
♣ 9 6 3                     ♣ 8 2
              ♠ A K 10
              ♥ K Q 3
              ♦ K 8 2
              ♣ K Q 5 4
```

West leads the ♠4 against 3NT and you win East's jack with the ace. Your remaining K-10 is a double stopper in the suit if West gains the lead. Since West surely holds the ♠Q, the K-10 will be only a single stopper if East gains the lead. You have six top tricks. Which red suit should you play first in your quest for three more tricks?

If the red aces are split and you happen to play the suit where West holds the ace, all will be well. By good fortune you will have 'attacked the entry to the danger hand'. West will not be able to continue spades safely when he takes his ace and you will have time to knock out the other red ace. However, that involves guesswork.

Since you have seven cards in diamonds and only six in hearts, it is better to play on diamonds first. You will then make the contract not only when West happens to hold the diamond ace but also when the suit breaks 3-3 and yields three tricks. You are still relying on good fortune, however. Is there some play that will guarantee the contract, however the cards lie?

Indeed there is. You must play diamonds in such a way that you do not need a 3-3 break in the suit. At Trick 2 cross to dummy with a club and lead a low diamond towards your king. Whatever happens on this trick, you will make the contract. First, West may hold the diamond ace. (If he wins, he cannot attack spades and you can play hearts when you regain the lead. If he ducks, you will switch to hearts immediately.) Second, East may hold the diamond ace and rise with the card. You will then have three diamond tricks, enough for the contract. Third, East may hold the diamond ace and duck. With one diamond trick safely collected, you can switch to hearts and score two more there.

Here is another situation where the defender gives you a trick if he rises:

```
         ♣ A J 5 4
                  N
♣ 9 6 3       W       E    ♣ K 10 7 2
                  S
         ♣ Q 8
```

You lead low from dummy. If East rises with the king you have three club tricks. If instead he plays low, you pocket a trick with the queen and switch elsewhere. (When East holds king third, you can score three club tricks by force. If he ducks on the first round, ace and another club will bring down the king.)

Here is another deal on the same theme. You cannot guarantee the contract this time but by playing the right suit — in the correct way — you can at least give yourself a chance.

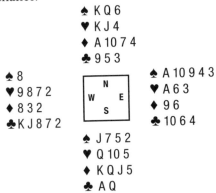

```
                  ♠ K Q 6
                  ♥ K J 4
                  ♦ A 10 7 4
                  ♣ 9 5 3
    ♠ 8                          ♠ A 10 9 4 3
    ♥ 9 8 7 2      N             ♥ A 6 3
    ♦ 8 3 2      W   E           ♦ 9 6
    ♣ K J 8 7 2    S             ♣ 10 6 4
                  ♠ J 7 5 2
                  ♥ Q 10 5
                  ♦ K Q J 5
                  ♣ A Q
```

BY THE WAY

If the ♠A was held by West, instead of East, the winning play would be to lead a low spade from the South hand. Since West holds five clubs to his partner's three, in the situation you fear, it is more likely that East will hold the spade length and therefore the ace of the suit.

West leads the ♣7 against 3NT and East plays the ten. This time you have no chance of a third stopper in the suit led. How should you play?

If you play hearts first, you risk going down whichever defender holds the ♥A. They can take the heart ace immediately and clear the club suit. You will have only eight top tricks and as soon as you play a spade the defenders will swoop with the ace and claim five tricks.

It's natural to play spades first, because that is the longer suit. Once again you must do so in such a way that a defender may have to pay a heavy price if he takes the ace on the first round. Cross to the ♦10 at Trick 2 and lead the ♠6. As on the last deal, if East rises with the ace you will have three spade tricks for a total of nine. If instead he plays low, you will pocket a trick with the ♠J and switch to hearts to set up the two extra tricks you need.

Summary

✓ When you have two stoppers to remove (or may have, if a finesse is wrong), attack first the entry to the danger hand.

✓ When you have two aces to knock out, it is often best to lead a low card through the defender who you do not want to gain the lead. If he rises, he may give you an extra trick. If he does not, you can win the trick and switch to the other suit.

CHOOSING WHICH SUIT TO PLAY

NOW TRY THESE...

1)

    ♠ A 9 4
    ♥ A 8 3
    ♦ Q J 6
    ♣ K 10 8 3

```
      N
  W       E
      S
```

    ♠ K 7 5
    ♥ K 9 4
    ♦ A 5 4
    ♣ Q J 5 2

West leads the ♥5 against 3NT. Plan the play.

2)

    ♠ 8 5
    ♥ A 7 3
    ♦ A J 10 9 3
    ♣ J 10 6

```
      N
  W       E
      S
```

    ♠ A K 4
    ♥ J 9 8 5
    ♦ K 8 4
    ♣ K Q 4

West leads the ♣6 against 3NT. Plan the play.

3)

    ♠ 7 6 3
    ♥ Q 10 2
    ♦ Q J 7 3
    ♣ K Q 5

```
      N
  W       E
      S
```

    ♠ A Q 4 2
    ♥ A K J 5
    ♦ K 6
    ♣ J 10 8

East opens the bidding with 1♠ and West leads the ♠5 against your eventual contract of 3NT, East playing the ♠8. Plan the play.

ANSWERS

1) You have only five top tricks and may therefore need extra tricks from both diamonds and clubs to bring your total to nine. You should win the heart lead immediately (just in case the defenders might otherwise take their heart trick and switch to spades). Suppose you play clubs next and East holds the ace. He will clear the hearts and you will probably go down if the diamond finesse loses. A better idea is to attack first the potential entry to the danger hand. Win the heart lead in dummy and run the queen of diamonds. If West wins and plays another heart you will win (or duck and win the third round of hearts — it makes no difference) and play clubs. Now, in the dangerous case where hearts are 5-2, East will have no heart to play when he wins with the club ace. Playing in this way, you will go down only when West holds five hearts, the ♦K and the ♣A.

2) Suppose you win the second spade and play diamonds, misguessing who holds the queen. The defenders will clear the spade suit and you will now go down when West holds the ace of clubs. A better idea is to play clubs first. If the defenders win with the ace and persist with spades, you will win and take the diamond finesse into the safe (East) hand. You don't mind the finesse losing, since East will have no spade to return unless the suit is 4-4 and poses no threat anyway.

   Let's suppose instead that East ducks the ♣K, wins the ♣Q and clears the clubs (the suit breaking 5-2). You will then run the ♦J into the safe (West) hand. As you see, East is the safe hand when West's spades are cleared; West is the safe hand when East's clubs are cleared.

3) You have six top tricks and must establish three more. It is no good playing a club, since East will win and clear the spade suit. When he later gains the lead with the diamond ace he will add three spade tricks to his two aces. Suppose you play the ♦K instead. That's no good either! East will win and clear the spades. You will score only two diamond tricks to go with your six winners in the majors. Only one play is good enough. You must cross to dummy with the ♥10 and lead a diamond towards the king.

   If East rises with the ace, you will score three diamond tricks. (You will cash the diamond king and reach the queen and jack of diamonds in dummy by overtaking the jack of hearts with the queen.) If instead East plays low on the first round of diamonds, you will pocket the diamond trick and play clubs to establish the two extra tricks that you need.

KEEPING TRUMP CONTROL

 Very little can be written as to the declarer's play of the 26 cards he has under his charge; it must necessarily be left a good deal to such individual intelligence as he may happen to possess.
W. Dalton. *Practical Bridge. 1908*

One of the advantages of playing in a suit contract, as opposed to notrump, is that you can use your trumps to prevent the opponents from scoring tricks in their strongest suit. This advantage is lost when you run out of trumps and the defenders regain the lead, proceeding to cash winners in their strong suit. You are then said to have lost **trump control**.

Let's start with a deal where many players would indeed lose trump control.

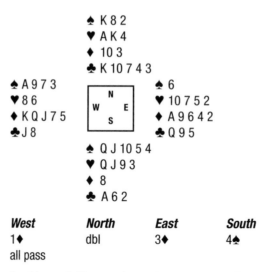

	♠ K 8 2	
	♥ A K 4	
	♦ 10 3	
	♣ K 10 7 4 3	

♠ A 9 7 3   ♠ 6
♥ 8 6   ♥ 10 7 5 2
♦ K Q J 7 5   ♦ A 9 6 4 2
♣ J 8   ♣ Q 9 5

              ♠ Q J 10 5 4
              ♥ Q J 9 3
              ♦ 8
              ♣ A 6 2

West	*North*	*East*	*South*
1♦	dbl	3♦	4♠
all pass			

West leads the king of diamonds against your spade game and continues with a second diamond. By leading his own strongest suit, he hopes to mount an attack on your trump holding, perhaps ending with more trumps than you. How will you play the contract?

Let's suppose first that you ruff the second diamond and play a trump. If West is a skillful defender, he will refuse to win with the ace. Why is that? Because he can see that a third round of diamonds would not then be profitable for the defenders. You would be able to ruff it in dummy, preserving your own trump length. Suppose you now lead a second round of trumps. West will duck again, for exactly the same reason. When West wins the third round of trumps, this will be the position:

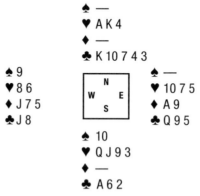

	♠ —	
	♥ A K 4	
	♦ —	
	♣ K 10 7 4 3	

♠ 9   ♠ —
♥ 8 6   ♥ 10 7 5
♦ J 7 5   ♦ A 9
♣ J 8   ♣ Q 9 5

              ♠ 10
              ♥ Q J 9 3
              ♦ —
              ♣ A 6 2

Now a diamond continuation will inflict serious damage. You will have to ruff in the long-trump hand, with your last trump. You will then have lost trump control. West will soon be able to ruff and cash his remaining diamonds.

What could you have done about it? It was no good switching to the side suits while you still had the J-10 of trumps to West's A-9. He would ruff with the nine at some stage and score two trump tricks to go with a club and a diamond.

No, there was only one way to make the contract and the key moment occurred back at Trick 2, when West led a second round of diamonds. Instead of weakening your trump holding by ruffing, you should have thrown a club. This would cost you nothing because your third club was a loser anyway. Do you see the point of this play? If West persists with a third round of diamonds, you will be able to ruff in the dummy — the hand with the shorter trumps. Since you will then still hold five trumps in your own hand (to West's four), you won't mind if West holds up the ace of trumps for two rounds before forcing you again in diamonds. You will be able to ruff, draw trumps and make ten tricks.

BY THE WAY

In this context, the word 'force' means 'force declarer to ruff'. The defenders are said to 'play a forcing game' when they keep leading their strongest suit, hoping to shorten declarer's trumps and make him lose trump control.

The risk of a damaging force may affect the way that you draw trumps. This is another deal where many declarers would go wrong:

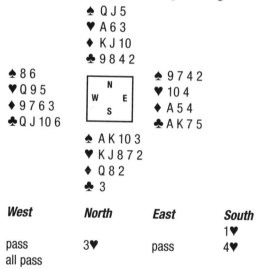

```
                    ♠ Q J 5
                    ♥ A 6 3
                    ♦ K J 10
                    ♣ 9 8 4 2
  ♠ 8 6                           ♠ 9 7 4 2
  ♥ Q 9 5           N             ♥ 10 4
  ♦ 9 7 6 3      W     E          ♦ A 5 4
  ♣ Q J 10 6        S             ♣ A K 7 5
                    ♠ A K 10 3
                    ♥ K J 8 7 2
                    ♦ Q 8 2
                    ♣ 3
```

West	North	East	South
			1♥
pass	3♥	pass	4♥
all pass			

The trumps are breaking 3-2, as you see, and perhaps you don't think there is any risk of losing control. West leads clubs and continues the suit, forcing you to ruff. Let's see what happens if you make the normal play in trumps, crossing to the ace and finessing the jack on the second round. West will win with the queen and force you again in clubs. You and West will then have one trump each. If you draw his trump before setting up the diamonds, East will be able to cash a club when you knock out the diamond ace. If instead you play diamonds before drawing the last trump, East will force your last trump (the king) by playing a fourth round of clubs. This will promote West's last trump and the effect will be the same — you will go down.

You cannot afford to take the trump finesse. If you play the ace and king of trumps instead, all is well. With two trumps remaining to West's one, you knock out the diamond ace. You ruff the club return, leaving yourself with the jack of trumps to West's queen. No matter. You simply play good cards in spades and diamonds, letting West score his master trump whenever he wishes. You have kept control and ten tricks are yours.

When you are playing in a 5-2 fit and the defenders have already forced you to ruff once, it is often right to draw two rounds of trumps and then turn to the side suits, leaving two trumps out. This deal is typical:

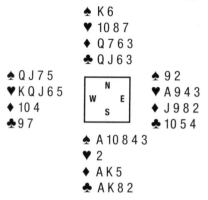

Five clubs might have been better but you alight in the spade game. West attacks in hearts and you ruff the second round. Unknown to you, West now holds the same trump length as you do. You are in danger of losing control. You draw two rounds of trumps with the king and ace. What next?

You have two trumps left (the 10-8), while the defenders hold the queen and jack. If the trumps started 3-3, you could score an overtrick by playing a third round of trumps. The queen and jack would fall together and you would be able to ruff the return and score the remaining tricks. This is a very dangerous way to play, though. If trumps are not 3-3, the defender who wins the third round of trumps will draw your last trump. You will then lose several heart tricks.

Instead of playing another round of trumps, you should abandon the trump suit and play your winners in the minor suits. The defenders will now score the queen and jack separately, whether or not the two trump honors lie in the same hand. More important, you will make the contract! You will lose one heart trick and two trump tricks.

There is one more technique that you can employ in the trump suit, when attempting to resist a forcing game. When you are likely to lose a trump trick you do so on an early round, while dummy's trumps can still protect you against the defenders' main suit. It is not easy to visualize, so let's look at a full deal illustrating the technique.

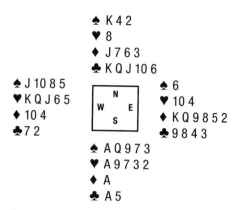

♠ K 4 2
♥ 8
♦ J 7 6 3
♣ K Q J 10 6

♠ J 10 8 5
♥ K Q J 6 5
♦ 10 4
♣ 7 2

♠ 6
♥ 10 4
♦ K Q 9 8 5 2
♣ 9 8 4 3

♠ A Q 9 7 3
♥ A 9 7 3 2
♦ A
♣ A 5

You bid to six spades and West leads the ♥K to your ace. How should you play the deal?

If trumps break 3-2, it is easy to make all thirteen tricks. You can score five tricks in each black suit, the two red aces and a heart ruff. So, you must look for a way to score twelve tricks when the trumps break 4-1. Suppose you play the king and ace of trumps, discovering that West started with four trumps. There will be no way to recover. If you surrender a trump to West now, he can cash heart tricks. If instead you ruff a heart and play the club winners, West will ruff before you have thrown all your hearts away.

What you need to do is to lose a trump trick at a time when the defenders can do no damage. Duck a round of trumps at Trick 2! Whatever the defenders return, you will take one heart ruff, draw trumps in three more rounds and make the remaining tricks. You will score four trump tricks, one heart ruff and seven winners in the side suits.

Perhaps you are saying 'Duck a trump at Trick 2? That's too difficult for me!' It is not at all difficult, once you think of it. Whenever you can afford to lose a trump trick and still make the contract, you should arrange to do so when the defenders can do no damage.

Sometimes you can avoid losing control by establishing a side suit before you draw trumps (while dummy can ruff the defenders' main suit.) Let's see a full deal where this technique would work well:

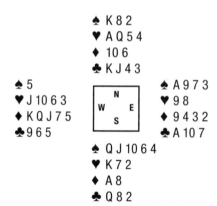

```
              ♠ K 8 2
              ♥ A Q 5 4
              ♦ 10 6
              ♣ K J 4 3
  ♠ 5                        ♠ A 9 7 3
  ♥ J 10 6 3       N         ♥ 9 8
  ♦ K Q J 7 5   W     E      ♦ 9 4 3 2
  ♣ 9 6 5          S         ♣ A 10 7
              ♠ Q J 10 6 4
              ♥ K 7 2
              ♦ A 8
              ♣ Q 8 2
```

West leads the ♦K against four spades. How will you play?

You win the second round of diamonds and play a trump to the king. Again we will assume that the defender in the East seat is a smart guy, who appreciates the value of holding up the trump ace. He ducks the first two rounds of trumps, West showing out on the second round. What now? If you play another trump East will win and force you with a diamond. After you ruff and draw East's last trump, you will have no trumps left. The defenders will be able to run their diamonds when you knock out the ♣A.

When West shows out on the second trump, you should abandon trumps for the moment and play clubs. East cannot damage you when he takes the ♣A, since a third diamond can be ruffed with dummy's last trump. When you regain the lead you will draw East's trumps and make the rest of the tricks.

BY THE WAY

Do you see why it was right to win the second round of diamonds rather than the first? Suppose East had held ♣A-x instead of ♣A-x-x. When you played clubs, he would win the second round and cross to partner's hand with a diamond to receive a club ruff. By ducking a diamond, you kill the only route to the West hand.

Summary

✓ When the defenders are playing a forcing game (leading their strongest suit to shorten your trump holding), you must sometimes discard from your hand until dummy can ruff the enemy suit. This preserves your own trump length.

✓ On other occasions you may have to refuse a trump finesse. If it were to lose, the defenders would have an extra chance to force you.

KEEPING TRUMP CONTROL

NOW TRY THESE...

1)

♠ A 9 8
♥ K 6 3
♦ 10 7 4
♣ J 10 8 2

West	North	East	South
			1♥
2♦	2♥	3♦	3♥
all pass			

♠ 7 5 4
♥ Q J 10 8 4
♦ 6
♣ A K Q 5

West leads the ace of diamonds and continues the suit. Plan the play.

2)

♠ 10 5 3
♥ J 6 3
♦ Q 6 2
♣ A 10 7 3

♠ A K Q J 7
♥ 5 2
♦ K J 10 3
♣ K 4

The defenders lead three rounds of hearts against 4♠. Plan the play.

3)

♠ 8 3
♥ 6
♦ A K 7 6 3
♣ A Q J 10 7

♠ A K Q 7 2
♥ A 8 3 2
♦ 10 5
♣ K 6

West leads the ♥K against your small slam in spades. Plan the play.

ANSWERS

1) Suppose you ruff the second diamond in your hand and subsequently discover that East holds four trumps. You will go down against best defense. East will hold up the ace of trumps for two rounds and then force the long-trump hand with another diamond. You will lose control. To avoid this fate, you should discard spade losers from the South hand on the second and third round of diamonds. Since you can then ruff a fourth round of diamonds in the dummy, the defenders will be powerless. You can win any continuation and play a trump, maintaining trump control.

2) Since you have a certain loser in the diamond suit, you have to ruff the third heart. You draw trumps next and there will be no problem if the suit breaks 3-2. In that case you can simply draw all the trumps and establish the diamond suit.

   What if two rounds of trumps reveal a 4-1 break in the suit? You must then establish the diamonds while the stiff ♠10 is still in dummy to deal with a fourth round of hearts. If the defenders cleverly hold up the diamond ace, you must judge whether to continue diamonds (risking a diamond ruff) or to draw trumps (taking the risk that the defender who holds the diamond ace will have a heart or two to cash). Unless you have some reason to read the cards in a particular way, it will generally be best to persist with diamonds.

3) Suppose you take two heart ruffs, using the club king as an entry for the second ruff. The contract will then be at risk when you attempt to re-enter your hand with a minor-suit ruff. You will have to ruff low and West may then overruff and cash a heart. What if you try to draw trumps immediately instead? When trumps break 4-2 and you turn to the club suit, a defender may be able to ruff (and cash a heart) before you can discard all your losers.

   Since you can afford to lose a trump trick, you should do so at a time when the defenders cannot damage you. Duck a trump at Trick 2! A heart return will not help the defenders because you can ruff in the dummy. On any other return you will draw trumps and discard your losing hearts on dummy's club suit.

ELIMINATION PLAY

♥ The real science of bridge lies in being able to place the cards towards the end of the hand. **W. Dalton.** *Practical Bridge. 1908*

There are many suit combinations where your chances as declarer are greater if the defenders make the first play in the suit. Look at this spade position, for example:

♠ K 10 5

♠ Q 9 8 3   ♠ 6 4 2

♠ A J 7

If you tackle this suit yourself, you will have to guess the position of the queen in order to score three tricks. If either defender makes the first play, the situation is brighter and you are assured of three tricks.

♥ J 6 2

♥ 10 8 5   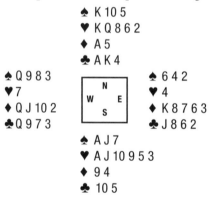   ♥ Q 9 7 4

♥ A K 3

If you play this suit yourself, the chances of three tricks are very poor. You would need to find one of the defenders with ♥Q-x. What if you can force East to make the first play in the heart suit? The odds improve greatly. You will score three tricks whenever East holds the queen.

It may not have occurred to you, but as declarer you *never* do better by playing a suit yourself. You will always do at least as well if the defenders make the first play.

So, how can you force the defenders to make the first play in a suit where you are hoping to avoid a loser? On many deals played in a suit contract it is possible. Let's place that first spade holding into a full deal:

♠ K 10 5
♥ K Q 8 6 2
♦ A 5
♣ A K 4

♠ Q 9 8 3   ♠ 6 4 2
♥ 7   ♥ 4
♦ Q J 10 2   ♦ K 8 7 6 3
♣ Q 9 7 3   ♣ J 8 6 2

♠ A J 7
♥ A J 10 9 5 3
♦ 9 4
♣ 10 5

West leads the ♦Q against six hearts. How should you play the slam?

Suppose you win the opening lead with the ♦A, draw trumps and take an immediate guess in spades. It will be an exciting moment, we grant you, but half the time you will go down.

An absolutely certain line of play is available. You must aim to make a defender win a diamond trick, forcing him to play a spade. Before doing this, you must remove any safe exit the defender might otherwise have. You draw trumps, removing the safe exit there. You then cash the two top clubs and ruff dummy's last club. This maneuver has left you without any clubs in your hand or the dummy. You have **stripped** the clubs, or **eliminated** the clubs. The defenders cannot now play a club safely as it would give you a ruff-and-sluff. You will be able to ruff the club in dummy, and at the same time discard (sluff) one of your losing spades from hand. This is the position:

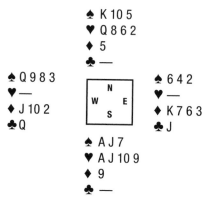

♠ K 10 5
♥ Q 8 6 2
♦ 5
♣ —

♠ Q 9 8 3
♥ —
♦ J 10 2
♣ Q

♠ 6 4 2
♥ —
♦ K 7 6 3
♣ J

♠ A J 7
♥ A J 10 9
♦ 9
♣ —

When you exit with a diamond, one or the other defender will find himself on lead. If he leads a spade next, you will be spared a guess in the suit. If instead he plays a diamond or a club, this will give you a ruff-and-sluff. Either way, you make the rest of the tricks.

The technique we have just seen is known as an **elimination play** because you eliminate one or more suits (removing the defenders' safe exits) before putting an opponent on lead. It is easy to perform and opportunities for it are frequent.

Here is another example:

BY THE WAY

The word 'strip' can also be used to mean 'remove the cards in a suit'. If you 'strip West's clubs', it means that you remove (or 'eliminate') West's clubs by playing sufficient rounds of the suit.

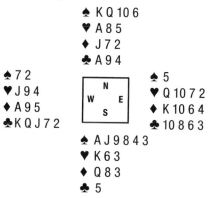

♠ K Q 10 6
♥ A 8 5
♦ J 7 2
♣ A 9 4

♠ 7 2
♥ J 9 4
♦ A 9 5
♣ K Q J 7 2

♠ 5
♥ Q 10 7 2
♦ K 10 6 4
♣ 10 8 6 3

♠ A J 9 8 4 3
♥ K 6 3
♦ Q 8 3
♣ 5

West leads the king of clubs against your game in spades. You have one loser in hearts and may lose three more tricks in diamonds if you have to play the suit yourself. What is your plan?

Your plan should be: 'I will draw trumps, eliminate clubs and then play ace, king and another heart, putting the defenders on lead. They will have to make the first play in diamonds, guaranteeing me a trick there, or concede a ruff-and-sluff.'

How does the play go? You win the club lead, draw trumps in two rounds and ruff a club. You cross to dummy's ♥A and ruff another club, eliminating the suit. You then play king and another heart. It makes no difference which defender wins the third round of hearts. He will have to make the first play in diamonds or give you a ruff-and-sluff.

Note that you must have at least one trump in each hand when you perform the throw-in. If you had trumps only in one hand, the defenders could exit in an eliminated suit without giving you a ruff-and-sluff.

Putting a particular defender on lead

Until now, you have not minded which defender won the trick when you surrendered the lead. Sometimes an elimination play will succeed only if a particular defender can be thrown in. Look at this deal:

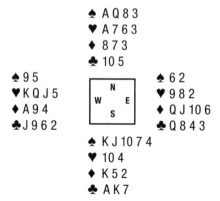

West leads the ♥K against your spade game. You have a certain loser in hearts and if you have to play diamonds yourself you are likely to lose three more tricks whenever West holds the ♦A. What can you do about it?

You must aim to put West on lead with the fourth round of hearts, discarding a diamond loser on the trick. You cannot afford to have East gain the lead as you prepare for the throw-in, so duck the ♥K at Trick 1 (just in case East holds the ♥J). You win the next heart, draw trumps in two rounds and ruff a heart in the South hand. Next you eliminate the clubs, by playing the ace and king and ruffing the third round. These cards will be left:

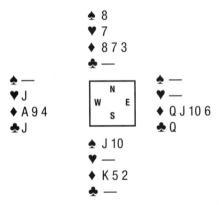

                    ♠ 8
                    ♥ 7
                    ♦ 8 7 3
                    ♣ —
    ♠ —   ♠ —
    ♥ J   ♥ —
    ♦ A 9 4   ♦ Q J 10 6
    ♣ J   ♣ Q
                    ♠ J 10
                    ♥ —
                    ♦ K 5 2
                    ♣ —

With the preparation complete, you lead dummy's last heart. East shows out, you are pleased to see, and you throw a diamond loser from your hand. West wins the trick and is endplayed. A diamond return will let you make your king, and a club return will give you a ruff-and-sluff.

As you see, it would have been no good to put East on lead. He would then have been able to lead a diamond through the king. West was your intended target for the throw-in and all went well because he was the defender who held the last heart. The play is called a **loser-on-loser elimination**. Here you threw one loser (a diamond) on another loser (dummy's last heart). Swapping one loser for another did not save you a trick directly, of course. The benefit came because West had to give you a trick with his return.

Sometimes you can put a defender on lead in the key suit itself:

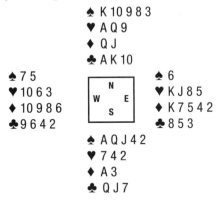

                    ♠ K 10 9 8 3
                    ♥ A Q 9
                    ♦ Q J
                    ♣ A K 10
    ♠ 7 5   ♠ 6
    ♥ 10 6 3   ♥ K J 8 5
    ♦ 10 9 8 6   ♦ K 7 5 4 2
    ♣ 9 6 4 2   ♣ 8 5 3
                    ♠ A Q J 4 2
                    ♥ 7 4 2
                    ♦ A 3
                    ♣ Q J 7

You reach a small slam in spades and are off to a great start when West's ♦10 lead reveals that you will have no diamond loser. What next?

If you play the hearts yourself, you will lose two heart tricks. By using an elimination play you can guarantee the contract (which you couldn't have done if West's opening lead had been a heart). You win the diamond lead and draw trumps. You then play your winners in the minor suits, reaching this position:

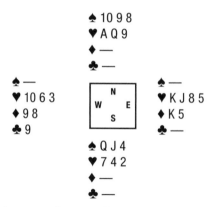

You play a heart to the nine, losing to the jack, but East has no good return. He must lead into dummy's ♥A-Q or give you a ruff-and-sluff.

What if West rises with the ♥10 on the first round, hoping to prevent his partner from being thrown in? You will cover with the queen and East will again be endplayed when he wins with the king. He will have to lead from the ♥J into dummy's ♥A-9 or concede a ruff-and-sluff.

Summary

✓ When you have plenty of trumps in both hands, think of an **elimination play**. You draw trumps, eliminate one or two side suits and then put a defender on lead. He will have to play one of your remaining suits, to your advantage, or give you a ruff-and-sluff.

✓ Sometimes you can put a defender on lead in the key suit itself. For example, with A-Q-9, you lead to the nine.

✓ When you need to put a particular defender on lead, you may be able to use a **loser-on-loser elimination**. You lead a card that only that defender can win, throwing a loser from the opposite hand.

ELIMINATION PLAY

NOW TRY THESE...

1)

    ♠ Q J 8 5
    ♥ 9 7 2
    ♦ K 10 4
    ♣ K 9 3

```
      N
   W     E
      S
```

    ♠ A K 10 7 4
    ♥ A 5 4
    ♦ Q 9 6
    ♣ A 2

West leads the ♥K against four spades. Plan the play. (Trumps are 3-1).

2)

    ♠ A 7
    ♥ K 6 2
    ♦ K 10 9 6 3
    ♣ A J 10

```
      N
   W     E
      S
```

    ♠ K 8 3
    ♥ A 3
    ♦ A Q 8 7 2
    ♣ 7 6 2

West leads the ♥J against six diamonds. Plan the play. (Trumps are 2-1).

3)

    ♠ Q J 3 2
    ♥ 5 4 2
    ♦ A K 7 6
    ♣ K 3

```
      N
   W     E
      S
```

    ♠ A K 10 9 6 4
    ♥ A Q 7
    ♦ 8 5
    ♣ A 4

West leads the ♣Q against your small slam in spades. Plan the play.
(Trumps are 2-1).

ANSWERS

1) If you play the diamond suit yourself, you will make the contract only if you can guess which defender holds the jack of diamonds. A better idea (surprise, surprise!) is to use elimination play. Win the heart lead and draw trumps. You then eliminate the club suit by playing the ace and king and ruffing the third round. Finally you exit in hearts. The opponents are welcome to their two tricks in this suit. They will then have to make the first play in the diamond suit or give you a ruff-and-sluff. Either way, you will lose only two hearts and one diamond.

2) If you play the club suit yourself, you risk losing two tricks when East holds the king and queen (both finesses will fail). Instead you should eliminate all the suits except clubs and play a club to the jack, endplaying East. How does the play go? Win the heart lead with the ace and draw trumps. Play the two top spades and ruff a spade in dummy, eliminating that suit. You then play the king of hearts and ruff a heart, eliminating that suit too. When you play a club to the jack, losing to the queen, East will have no good return when he wins. He will either have to lead a club into dummy's ♣A-10 or give you a ruff-and-sluff.

3) The problem suit is hearts. Suppose you draw trumps, eliminate both the minor suits and lead a low heart from dummy. By inserting the jack, ten, nine or eight, East can prevent you from playing the seven and ducking the trick to West. In that case you will make the contract only when the heart king is onside. A better idea is to aim for a loser-on-loser elimination on the fourth round of diamonds. Win the club lead with the ace, draw trumps and play the ace and king of diamonds. Ruff one diamond in your hand and return to dummy with the king of clubs. You then lead the fourth round of diamonds. If East shows out, all is well. You will throw a heart loser from your hand, allowing West to win the trick. He will then have to lead a heart into the A-Q or give you a ruff-and-sluff.

   What if East produces the last diamond? Nothing has been lost. You will ruff in your hand, cross to dummy with a third round of trumps and lead a heart. If East carelessly plays a card lower than the seven, or if West was dealt something like K-J-10, you will be able to duck the trick to West. As before, he will be endplayed.

THE HOLD-UP PLAY IN A SUIT CONTRACT

 If you hold a master card, hold it up until you are sure that the leader's partner has not another one to put him in with.
W. Dalton. *Practical Bridge. 1908*

In Chapter 5 we saw the importance of the hold-up play in notrump. There are several situations where you can hold up an ace to good effect, even when playing in a suit contract. The reason may be the same as in notrump — you want to break the communication between the two defenders. Look at this deal:

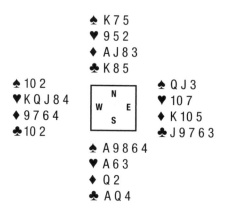

              ♠ K 7 5
              ♥ 9 5 2
              ♦ A J 8 3
              ♣ K 8 5

♠ 10 2   ♠ Q J 3
♥ K Q J 8 4   N   ♥ 10 7
♦ 9 7 6 4   W   E   ♦ K 10 5
♣ 10 2   S   ♣ J 9 7 6 3

              ♠ A 9 8 6 4
              ♥ A 6 3
              ♦ Q 2
              ♣ A Q 4

West leads the ♥K against your game in spades. Suppose that you win the first trick with the ace. You draw two rounds of trumps with the ace and king, pleased to see the suit divide 3-2. When you run the queen of diamonds, your luck changes. East wins with the king, cashes the trump queen and returns a heart. Two heart tricks bring the defenders' total to four. Down one!

To give yourself an extra chance you should hold up the ace of hearts for one round, winning the heart continuation. As before, you draw two rounds of trumps and run the queen of diamonds. East wins but he now has no heart to return. When you regain the lead you will play the ace and jack of diamonds, throwing the heart loser. You see the difference? By ducking one round of hearts, you were able to break the communication between the two defenders. You took advantage of the extra chance that hearts might divide 5-2.

Another reason to duck the opening lead is to keep a particular defender off lead. On the next deal East is the danger hand:

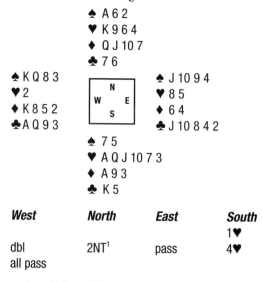

              ♠ A 6 2
              ♥ K 9 6 4
              ♦ Q J 10 7
              ♣ 7 6

♠ K Q 8 3   ♠ J 10 9 4
♥ 2   N   ♥ 8 5
♦ K 8 5 2   W   E   ♦ 6 4
♣ A Q 9 3   S   ♣ J 10 8 4 2

              ♠ 7 5
              ♥ A Q J 10 7 3
              ♦ A 9 3
              ♣ K 5

West	North	East	South
			1♥
dbl	2NT[1]	pass	4♥
all pass			

1.   North would have made a limit raise of 3♥ without the double.

West leads the ♠K against your heart game. Let's first see what may happen if you win the first trick with the ace. East will play the ♠J, to show his honor sequence in the suit. You draw trumps in two rounds and run the diamond queen, losing to the king. West will now lead a low spade to put his partner on play and a club switch, through the king, defeats the game.

You can prevent such a defense by ducking the ♠K at Trick 1. Do you see the difference this makes? You win the next spade, draw trumps and run the ♦Q to the king. West cannot now reach his partner's hand for a club lead. He may well play ace and another club, in the desperate hope that his partner holds the club king. If instead he exits passively in spades or diamonds, you will simply discard one of your clubs on the fourth round of diamonds.

Sometimes you duck at Trick 1 because you want to keep your left-hand opponent off lead. Many players would go wrong here:

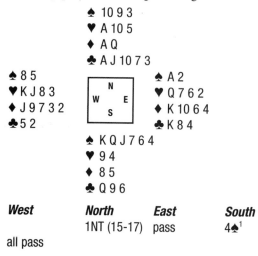

	♠ 10 9 3	
	♥ A 10 5	
	♦ A Q	
	♣ A J 10 7 3	
♠ 8 5		♠ A 2
♥ K J 8 3		♥ Q 7 6 2
♦ J 9 7 3 2		♦ K 10 6 4
♣ 5 2		♣ K 8 4
	♠ K Q J 7 6 4	
	♥ 9 4	
	♦ 8 5	
	♣ Q 9 6	

West	North	East	South
	1NT (15-17)	pass	4♠[1]
all pass			

1. Obviously this pair do not play transfers.

West leads the ♥3 against your game in spades. Once again we will suppose first that you win immediately with dummy's ace. When you play a trump, East will win with the ace and play a heart to partner's king. Your contract is now at risk. If West switches to a diamond, he will set up his partner's king before you have established a discard on the clubs. You would then lose a trick in each suit, going down one.

How can you do better? The best solution is to play low from dummy at Trick 1. East (the safe hand, who cannot attack diamonds) wins with the ♥Q. You win the heart return and play trumps. When East takes the ace he cannot cross to his partner's hand. You will win whatever he leads, draw the outstanding trumps and run the ♣Q. Your diamond loser will eventually be thrown on dummy's clubs.

Another reason to hold up an ace at Trick 1 is to prepare for a ruff. What do you make of this deal?

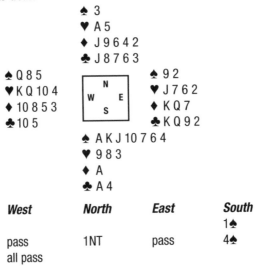

```
                    ♠ 3
                    ♥ A 5
                    ♦ J 9 6 4 2
                    ♣ J 8 7 6 3
    ♠ Q 8 5                        ♠ 9 2
    ♥ K Q 10 4         N           ♥ J 7 6 2
    ♦ 10 8 5 3      W     E        ♦ K Q 7
    ♣ 10 5            S            ♣ K Q 9 2
                    ♠ A K J 10 7 6 4
                    ♥ 9 8 3
                    ♦ A
                    ♣ A 4
```

West	North	East	South
			1♠
pass	1NT	pass	4♠
all pass			

West leads the ♥K against your game in spades. What are the prospects? You have four potential losers — one in trumps, two in hearts and one in clubs. A heart ruff in dummy would be welcome but the opponents may be able to remove dummy's trump before you take the ruff. Suppose you win the opening lead with dummy's ♥A and play another heart. If East is awake, he will rise with the heart jack and lead a trump through your holding. Whether or not you opt to finesse, you will go down. What else can you try?

Try the effect of holding up dummy's ace of hearts at Trick 1, allowing West's king to win. If he plays any side suit next, you will be able to score a heart ruff. If instead he switches to a trump, he will surrender his trick in the suit. Ten tricks, whatever West does!

Summary

✓ Even in a suit contract it can be worthwhile to hold up an ace. By doing so, you may break the defenders' communication.

✓ When a king is led, a hold-up may prevent the other defender from gaining the lead later. When a low card is led, a hold-up may prevent the opening leader from regaining the lead.

THE HOLD-UP PLAY IN A SUIT CONTRACT

NOW TRY THESE...

1)

    ♠ 8 3
    ♥ 10 4
    ♦ 10 7 5 3
    ♣ K J 9 6 2

    ♠ A 10
    ♥ K Q J 9 6 2
    ♦ K 2
    ♣ A Q 5

West (who opened 1♠) leads the ♠Q against 4♥. How will you play the hand?

2)

    ♠ 9 5
    ♥ 10 6 2
    ♦ A 9 6 3
    ♣ K 10 7 3

       N
   W   E
       S

    ♠ K Q J 8 6 4
    ♥ A 7
    ♦ K 8
    ♣ A 8 4

You reach 4♠ after East has opened with a weak 2♥ (showing six hearts and 6-10 points). How will you play the hand when West leads the ♥8?

3)

    ♠ 9 8 5 3
    ♥ A 2
    ♦ A 7 6 4
    ♣ A J 3

       N
   W   E
       S

    ♠ K Q J 10 6 2
    ♥ K 6
    ♦ 8 5 3
    ♣ Q 8

West leads the ♦Q against your spade game. How will you play the hand?

ANSWERS

1) Suppose you win the ♠Q lead with the ace. When West wins a trump lead with the ace, he will be able to cross to his partner's ♠K. East can then lead through your ♦K to defeat the game — West surely has the ♦A for his opening bid. Since East is the danger hand (the defender who can lead through your ♦K), you must aim to keep him off lead. You can do this by ducking the ♠Q opening lead. West will then have no route to his partner's hand when he wins with the trump ace.

   You may wonder what would happen if East played the king of spades on his partner's queen at Trick 1. If you were to duck then, a diamond switch would beat the contract. Instead, you should win with the ace. Your ♠10 would prevent West from crossing in spades later in the play.

2) East's opening weak two-bid tells you that West almost certainly holds two hearts to his partner's six. Suppose you win the heart lead with the ace and play the king of trumps. If West wins from ♠A-10-x, he will be able to lead his second heart to partner's hand. A third round of hearts will then promote West's ten of trumps. (If you ruff high, West's ♠10 will become good and you will still have a club loser. If instead you throw a club, East will continue with another heart to promote the ♠10.) To break the defenders' communications you should hold up the ♥A at Trick 1. When West wins with the ace of trumps he will have no way to reach his partner's hand for that deadly heart lead through.

3) You are in danger of losing two diamonds, the ♣K and the ace of trumps. The best chance is to play West for four diamonds. You duck the first round of diamonds and win the second. When you play trumps you must hope that East has the ace. If the diamond suit is indeed divided 4-2, he will then have no diamond to play. You can win his return, draw trumps and run the club queen. If this loses, you will be able to discard your remaining diamond loser on the third round of clubs.

   (If West has led from ♦Q-J-10-x-x, with East holding a singleton ♦K, it makes no difference to the fate of the contract whether you win the opening lead or not.)

THE THROW-IN AT NOTRUMP

 It is sometimes necessary, in order to make a contract, to place certain cards in one hand or the other and play as if you knew they were there. When this is the case, make up your mind and go for it boldly. ***W. Dalton.*** *Practical Bridge. 1908*

In Chapter 16 we looked at elimination play in a suit contract. By eliminating one or more side suits (in other words, removing the holdings from your hand and the dummy) and putting a defender on lead, you were able to force him to give you a trick. The important feature was that he could not play one of the eliminated suits without conceding a ruff-and-sluff. In this chapter we will look at a similar play, most often performed at notrump. Again the idea is to put a defender on lead at a time when he will have to give you a trick.

Since the ruff-and-sluff element is not present this time (you are playing in notrump) it is not so easy to ensure that a defender has no safe exit cards. Suppose you have a side suit of A-x opposite K-x in a suit contract, with trumps still in both hands. You simply play the ace and king and a defender cannot then safely play that suit — he would give you a ruff-and-sluff. In notrump, of course, he could still play the suit. Indeed, he would score tricks there, since your stoppers would be gone! Playing in notrump, you can eliminate a defender's safe exit cards in a suit only by removing all *his* cards in that suit. It is irrelevant whether you still have some cards left in the suit yourself.

This may sound a bit dry, we realize. Let's look at an example:

```
                    ♠ 8 7 5 2
                    ♥ 8 4
                    ♦ A 7 5
                    ♣ A K 10 4
    ♠ K 6 3                            ♠ J 10 9 4
    ♥ K Q J 10 3        N             ♥ 9 7
    ♦ Q 9 2         W       E         ♦ 10 8 6 4
    ♣ 7 3              S             ♣ 9 6 5
                    ♠ A Q
                    ♥ A 6 5 2
                    ♦ K J 3
                    ♣ Q J 8 2
```

West	North	East	South
			1NT (15-17)
pass	2♣	pass	2♥
pass	3NT	all pass	

BY THE WAY

Do you see why it would have been no good to win the first heart, strip West's clubs and exit with the second round of hearts? It's because East might have won the trick. He could then lead through your spade holding. It was not even safe to win the second heart and exit with a third heart. If the hearts were divided 4-3, East might still win the third round. It is West that you need to have on lead.

West leads the king of hearts against 3NT. How do you plan to make nine tricks?

You can count eight top tricks and a successful finesse in spades or diamonds would bring the total to nine. However, it is dangerous to take one of these finesses. If it happens to lose, West may cash enough hearts to beat the contract. What else can you try?

You should duck the first two hearts and win the third, East showing out. You plan now to put West on lead with a heart, forcing him to lead into one of your tenaces. How about throwing him in now, at Trick 3? That's no good. After cashing his hearts, he would have a safe exit in clubs. Before putting West in, you must remove his clubs. You play the ace, king and queen of clubs, West discarding a spade on the third round.

You have stripped West's clubs and the time has come to play a heart, on which dummy throws a spade. West wins and cashes his last heart. This causes you no problem. You throw another spade from the dummy and a club from your hand. West will then scratch his head, wondering what to play next. It makes no difference. He will have to give you a ninth trick by playing either a spade or a diamond.

As you see, the play is closely related to elimination play in a suit contract. You took away West's safe exit in clubs, by removing all his clubs, and then put him on lead. He was then forced to give you a trick in one of your problem suits.

Perhaps you think that the play was possible only because West held just four (heart) winners in his hand. Strange to relate, you can often succeed when the opening lead has set up more than four winners in the leader's hand. The play is a little more difficult than on many of the deals we have seen so far in the book. Still, only the brightest of students will have stayed with us until Chapter 18… so that should be no problem.

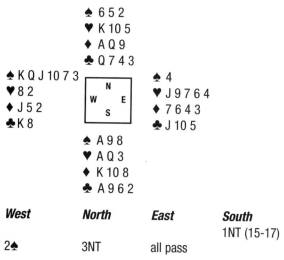

West	North	East	South
			1NT (15-17)
2♠	3NT	all pass	

West leads the king of spades and continues the suit. You win the second round, noting that West started with six spades. You have eight top tricks and need an extra trick from the club suit. West's overcall strongly suggests that he holds the ♣K. What can you do?

It is no good simply removing West's five red cards and throwing him in with a spade. He would have five spade tricks to cash! Instead you should play all six winners in the red suits. West will not enjoy the sixth red card at all. If he discards one of his precious spade winners, you will be able to throw him in, forcing him to lead from the ♣K (he will have only four spade winners left to take). If instead he discards the ♣8, your ace of clubs will drop his king. The play is not that difficult, in fact. If West refuses to discard a spade, your only chance is that the club king has been unguarded and will fall under the ace.

The bidding will often guide you towards a throw-in. Look at this deal:

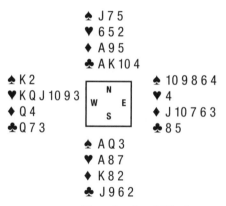

♠ J 7 5
♥ 6 5 2
♦ A 9 5
♣ A K 10 4

♠ K 2
♥ K Q J 10 9 3
♦ Q 4
♣ Q 7 3

♠ 10 9 8 6 4
♥ 4
♦ J 10 7 6 3
♣ 8 5

♠ A Q 3
♥ A 8 7
♦ K 8 2
♣ J 9 6 2

You play in 3NT after West opens 1♥. West attacks in hearts and you win the second round, East showing out. You finesse successfully in clubs and West throws a diamond on the fourth round of the suit. What next?

You have eight top tricks and will need an extra trick from the spade suit. Taking a spade finesse through East is against the odds, because West's opening bid makes him a favorite to hold the ♠K. Aim instead for a throw-in on West, forcing him to lead away from the ♠K. How about throwing him in now? It is no good for two reasons: he would have five hearts to take, and also he could exit safely with the ♦Q. So, you play the ace and king of diamonds first. You remove West's safe diamond exit, and he will also have to throw a heart winner on the second diamond (or bare the ♠K). You can then throw him in with a heart, forcing a lead into your ♠A-Q.

Summary

✓ You can sometimes score an extra trick, even at notrump, by forcing a defender to lead into a tenace (a holding such as A-Q). Remove a defender's cards in the other side suits and then throw the defender in, forcing him to play the remaining suit.

✓ Even when a defender has five winners to take (against 3NT) he may have to discard one of them in order to keep his guard on your key suit. You will then be able to throw him in.

THE THROW-IN AT NOTRUMP

NOW TRY THESE...

1)

♠ 7 5 4
♥ 7 6 2
♦ Q J 6 5
♣ K 7 4

♠ A Q 6
♥ A 10 4
♦ A K 9 2
♣ A J 5

West leads the ♥K against 3NT. Plan the play.

2)

♠ 8 6
♥ Q J 6
♦ Q 6
♣ A K J 10 4 2

♠ A 7 4 3
♥ K 7 4
♦ A 7 3
♣ Q 9 3

West, who opened 1♠, leads the ♠5 against 3NT. East plays the queen. You allow this to win and East returns the ♠10. Plan the play.

3)

♠ Q 8 4
♥ 7 4 3
♦ Q 7
♣ Q J 10 8 6

♠ A 7 5
♥ A K 6
♦ A 6 5
♣ K 9 5 4

West, who opened 1♥, leads the heart queen against 3NT. Plan the play.

ANSWERS

1) You can count eight top tricks. A successful finesse in either clubs or spades would bring the total to nine, but that would rely on luck. A better idea is to plan a throw-in on West. Win the second heart and play the ace, king and queen of diamonds, which should exhaust West of the suit. Now exit with a heart. West is welcome to cash three more hearts. You will throw a spade and a diamond from the South hand, two spades from the dummy. West will then have to lead into one of your tenaces, giving you a ninth trick.

   If West surprises you by turning up with four diamonds, play a fourth round of diamonds and proceed with the throw-in anyway. You will still succeed when West started with K-Q-J-x of hearts. If he has five hearts, in addition to four diamonds, you will be embarrassed for a discard on the last heart. Best is to throw a club. If West defends accurately now, exiting with a club, win with the club ace and cross to dummy's king of clubs. You will have to take a spade finesse.

2) Duck the first and second rounds of spades and win the third round. West's opening bid marks him with the ace of hearts and the king of diamonds. When you play six rounds of clubs, throwing one card from each of the other three suits, West will have to discard a major-suit winner to retain his guard on the king of diamonds. You can then throw him in with a heart, forcing him to give you two diamonds at the end.

   If West discards a diamond or two, keeping enough major-suit winners to defeat the contract, you will have to play the ♦A instead, hoping that the ♦K is now singleton and will fall under the ace.

3) Win the first round of hearts and clear the club suit. West will win and return another heart. Win this trick too and play all your club winners. There are only fifteen points out, so it is quite likely that West holds both the ♠K and the ♦K. After removing West's clubs, you put him on lead with a heart. You hope then that he will have to lead away from one of his kings, giving you a ninth trick with the queen of that suit.

CHAPTER 19

REVERSING THE DUMMY

 On occasion, you may find it advantageous to conduct the play by taking ruffs in your own hand rather than the dummy's.
W. Dalton. *Practical Bridge. 1908*

When we looked at the subject of ruffing losers, way back in Chapter 2, we noted that you could score an extra trick by ruffing in the hand with fewer trumps. The trumps in the other hand (the long-trump hand) would score tricks anyway, so it would not help you to use them for ruffs. Look at this typical trump holding:

♥ A K 8

	N	
W		E
	S	

♥ Q J 10 9 2

You start with five trump tricks. If you take one ruff in the dummy, you increase this to six. Take two ruffs there and you will score a total of seven trump tricks. Suppose instead that you take a ruff or two in the South hand. How many trump tricks will you make? Just five — the same number that you started with.

However, if you can take *three* ruffs in the South hand, something strange happens. You make a total of six trump tricks! Three ruffs and three more rounds of trumps, ending in the dummy. In other words, it *can* be worthwhile to ruff in the long-trump hand, provided you take enough ruffs. What do we mean by 'enough ruffs'? We mean that the 'long-trump hand' will become the 'short-trump hand' after the ruffs have taken place. In this particular example you will have two trumps left in the South hand, after three ruffs, and three trumps in the North hand.

Taking such a large number of ruffs in the long-trump hand is known as **reversing the dummy**. You are treating declarer's hand as a dummy, by taking ruffs there. Let's see a full-deal example that features the trump holding we have just seen.

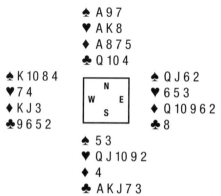

```
              ♠ A 9 7
              ♥ A K 8
              ♦ A 8 7 5
              ♣ Q 10 4
  ♠ K 10 8 4            ♠ Q J 6 2
  ♥ 7 4         N        ♥ 6 5 3
  ♦ K J 3    W     E     ♦ Q 10 9 6 2
  ♣ 9 6 5 2      S       ♣ 8
              ♠ 5 3
              ♥ Q J 10 9 2
              ♦ 4
              ♣ A K J 7 3
```

You bid to a grand slam in hearts (no half measures!) and West leads a trump. How can you make thirteen tricks?

Suppose you plan the contract in the traditional way, counting the losers in the long-trump hand (South). You have one loser in the spade suit and there is apparently no way to dispose of it.

Now try something different. Pretend that the South hand is dummy and that North is the declarer. What losers are there in the North hand? There are two spade losers and three diamond losers. Perhaps you can ruff all three diamond losers and eventually discard the two spade losers on South's club suit.

Let's try it. You win the trump lead in the South hand, cross to the ace of diamonds and take the first diamond ruff. A club to the queen is followed by a second diamond ruff and a spade to the ace. You ruff dummy's last diamond (all the ruffs were taken with high trumps), leaving this position:

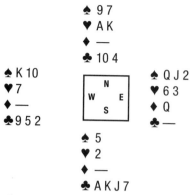

```
          ♠ 9 7
          ♥ A K
          ♦ —
          ♣ 10 4

♠ K 10              ♠ Q J 2
♥ 7        N        ♥ 6 3
♦ —     W     E     ♦ Q
♣ 9 5 2    S        ♣ —

          ♠ 5
          ♥ 2
          ♦ —
          ♣ A K J 7
```

You cross to the ace of trumps and draw the last trump with dummy's king. You then play four more rounds of clubs, throwing the two spade losers in dummy. Grand slam made!

That was a very unusual way of playing a hand — one that you would consider only when you could not make the contract in the traditional way. It is worth looking back at it for a moment. How many side-suit tricks did you take? Five clubs and two aces — a total of seven. You therefore needed six trump tricks to make the grand slam. You accomplished this by scoring three diamond ruffs in the South hand and by drawing three rounds of trumps, ending in the dummy.

Sometimes you take ruffs in the long-trump hand solely because your trumps are not strong enough to draw the adverse trumps. You therefore seek to score tricks with them by ruffing.

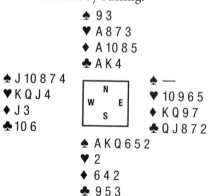

```
             ♠ 9 3
             ♥ A 8 7 3
             ♦ A 10 8 5
             ♣ A K 4

♠ J 10 8 7 4              ♠ —
♥ K Q J 4       N        ♥ 10 9 6 5
♦ J 3        W     E     ♦ K Q 9 7
♣ 10 6          S        ♣ Q J 8 7 2

             ♠ A K Q 6 5 2
             ♥ 2
             ♦ 6 4 2
             ♣ 9 5 3
```

With high hopes of defeating the contract, West leads the ♥K against your spade game. You win with dummy's ace and note that you have two diamond

REVERSING THE DUMMY

losers and one club loser. There's nothing you can do about any of those but as long as the trumps break 3-2, there will be no further loser. You play a trump to the ace and… oh no! East shows out. What now?

As well as the three side-suit losers, you now have two trump losers. It may not look very promising, but if you can score the three low trumps in your hand by ruffing you will score six trump tricks. Add the four winners in the side suits and the total — by some kind of magic — will come to ten.

You cross to the ace of clubs and ruff a heart with a low trump. A club to the king permits a second heart ruff with a low trump, West again following suit. You return to dummy for the last time with the ace of diamonds and lead a fourth rounds of hearts. You ruff with your last low trump and (yes!) West follows suit. Your three top trumps bring the total to ten tricks.

We said at the start that ruffing in the long-trump hand did not usually bring you extra tricks. Why did it do so on this occasion? Because your trumps were not strong enough to draw West's trumps when the suit broke 5-0. You therefore attempted to score the low trumps by ruffing.

Before we close the chapter we should mention one more thing about that last deal. You were lucky that dummy had three entries (♦A ♣A-K), so that you could lead hearts three times for a ruff in the South hand. What would have happened if, say, the ♦A had been in the South hand and you had one entry fewer to the dummy? Do you see the answer?

You would have had to make use of the entry to dummy at Trick 1, when you won with the ace of hearts. You would have had to ruff a heart at Trick 2, just in case the trumps were about to break badly and ruffs in the long-trump hand would be needed.

Summary

✓ When you have a side-suit shortage in the long-trump hand, and a contract seems to be impossible when planned from that hand, consider a 'dummy reversal'. In the classic variation of this play you take several ruffs in the long-trump hand, winding up with fewer trumps than dummy, and eventually drawing trumps from the dummy.

✓ A less common variation of the dummy reversal may occur when your trump honors are not strong enough to draw the defenders' trumps. You aim instead to score your low trumps by ruffing.

REVERSING THE DUMMY

NOW TRY THESE...

1)

♠ K J 7
♥ A Q
♦ A J 4 2
♣ A 9 7 3

♠ A Q 10 9 2
♥ 5 2
♦ K Q 10 9 7
♣ 6

West leads a trump against your grand slam in spades. Plan the play.

2)

♠ A 9 8
♥ K Q 7 4
♦ A 10 8
♣ A J 4

♠ 5
♥ A J 10 5
♦ 7 5 3 2
♣ K Q 10 7

West leads the ♠K against your small slam in hearts. Plan the play.

3)

♠ Q
♥ A 8 6 3
♦ A 8 7 4
♣ 9 8 4 2

♠ A K 7 5 3 2
♥ K 5 2
♦ 6
♣ A 7 3

West leads the ♦K against your spade game. Plan the play.

ANSWERS

1) If you plan the contract by considering the losers in the South hand, you will find one heart loser. You can dispose of this only with a successful finesse of dummy's queen. Is there anything better? Yes, if trumps break 3-2 you can perform a dummy reversal. Win the trump lead in the South hand, cross to dummy's ace of clubs and ruff a club. When you return to dummy with a second round of trumps, you will discover whether the trumps are 3-2. If they are, ruff another club, return to dummy with a diamond and ruff dummy's last club. You can then cross to the ace of hearts to draw the defenders' last trump, eventually discarding the ♥Q on the fifth round of diamonds. If instead the trumps break 4-1 a dummy reversal will not be possible. You will have to draw trumps and then take the heart finesse. Good luck!

2) If you plan the contract from the South hand, considering the losers there, you will conclude that prospects are not bright. It seems you are destined to lose two diamond tricks. Let's plan the contract by pretending that North is declarer and South is the dummy. The two spade losers can be ruffed and one of the two diamond losers can be thrown on South's club suit. That's better! Win the spade lead, ruff a spade low and play the ace and jack of trumps. It makes no difference if trumps have broken 4-1. Return to dummy with a club and ruff dummy's last spade. A diamond to the ace will allow you to draw the remaining trumps with dummy's K-Q. Finally you will play four rounds of clubs.

Remember this: Whenever you are in a 4-4 fit, with a shortage in your hand, check to see if prospects look better when considered from the dummy's point of view.

3) You have only four side-suit winners and must attempt to add six trump tricks. All will be easy if trumps break 3-3 but this is against the odds. If trumps break 4-2 or worse, you will need to score three of your low trumps by ruffing. Entries to dummy are sparse, so win the diamond lead and ruff a diamond at Trick 2. Cross to the queen of trumps and ruff another diamond. Now play the ace and king of trumps. If trumps break 3-3, you have ten easy tricks. Otherwise you will need another diamond ruff, to make your remaining low trump. Play the king and ace of hearts and lead dummy's last diamond, ruffing in your hand. (If trumps broke 4-2 and the last trump lies with East, you will make the contract even if he started with only three diamonds. He must either ruff with the top trump, setting up your last small trump, or allow you to take a ruff with it.)

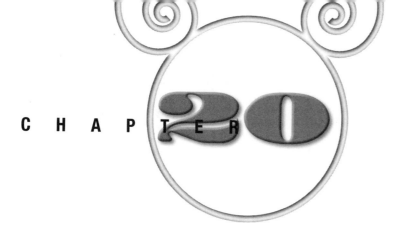

C H A P T E R **20**

COMBINING TWO CHANCES

When planning the play, it is usually right to prefer a line that combines two different chances rather than one that relies on a single chance. What do we mean by that? An example will make it clear:

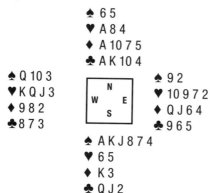

```
              ♠ 6 5
              ♥ A 8 4
              ♦ A 10 7 5
              ♣ A K 10 4
♠ Q 10 3                    ♠ 9 2
♥ K Q J 3        N          ♥ 10 9 7 2
♦ 9 8 2       W     E       ♦ Q J 6 4
♣ 8 7 3          S          ♣ 9 6 5
              ♠ A K J 8 7 4
              ♥ 6 5
              ♦ K 3
              ♣ Q J 2
```

West leads the ♥K against six spades. What is your plan?

You win the heart lead and must decide how to play the trumps. The normal play with this combination is to finesse the jack. That is the percentage play when considering the trump suit in isolation. It gives you a 34% chance of picking up the trump suit for no loser (half of the 68% for a 3-2 break). On this particular deal, though, the finesse is an all-or-nothing play. If it loses, West will cash a heart trick and you will go down.

BY THE WAY

It's true that when East holds Q-x-x-x in the trump suit you are better placed after a finesse. You can draw two more rounds of trumps and will then need East to follow to only three clubs. If instead you play for the drop in trumps, finding East with Q-x-x-x, you will need him to follow to four clubs (to avoid him ruffing with the low trump). Even so, playing for the drop in trumps is appreciably better overall.

What will happen if you make the second-best play in the trump suit instead, playing for the drop? You will have less chance of picking up the trumps (only 27%) but you will not be dead if this chance fails. If the defender left with the queen of trumps also holds at least three clubs, you can discard your heart loser on the fourth round of clubs. That adds another 20%, giving you a total of 47%. This makes the second line much better than the first.

Very few players, even experts, make this sort of detailed mathematical calculation at the table. The point to remember is that two chances are usually better than one.

The next deal offers an apparent choice of two finesses.

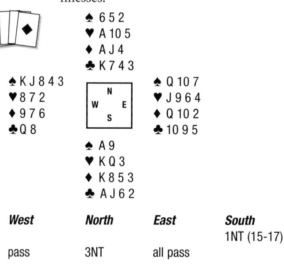

```
                  ♠ 6 5 2
                  ♥ A 10 5
                  ♦ A J 4
                  ♣ K 7 4 3
  ♠ K J 8 4 3                    ♠ Q 10 7
  ♥ 8 7 2          N             ♥ J 9 6 4
  ♦ 9 7 6       W     E          ♦ Q 10 2
  ♣ Q 8            S             ♣ 10 9 5
                  ♠ A 9
                  ♥ K Q 3
                  ♦ K 8 5 3
                  ♣ A J 6 2
```

West	North	East	South
			1NT (15-17)
pass	3NT	all pass	

West leads the ♠4 to East's queen, which you allow to win. When the spade ten is returned, you win with the ace and West plays the three. It seems that the spades are divided 5-3 (because West has shown one card below his fourth-best lead). The defenders will therefore be able to score a total of five tricks, beating the game, if they gain the lead. What is your best chance?

You can count eight top tricks and a successful finesse in either minor will give you a ninth trick. Should you rely on the diamond finesse, do you think, or the club finesse?

You should not rush to take *either* finesse! In this situation, where you have a choice of queen finesses, you should first play for the drop in one suit. By cashing the ace and king in one suit, you give yourself the chance that the queen will fall in two rounds. If the queen does not fall, you will take a finesse in the other suit. You will have combined two different chances — playing for the drop in one suit and taking a finesse in another.

Should you play the ace and king of clubs, or the ace and king of diamonds? Since you have eight clubs between the hands and only seven diamonds, there is more chance that the club queen will drop in two rounds. When the cards lie as in our diagram, the club queen does fall. If it failed to show in two rounds, you would take the diamond finesse.

The club queen will fall in two rounds about 30% of the time, so it is a huge additional chance. Often the extra chance will be smaller. You have, say, ♣A-x-x-x opposite ♣Q-x-x-x and you cash the ♣A, before taking a do-or-die finesse in another suit, just in case the ♣K is singleton. This is only a 6% chance. However, these extra-chance plays can make the difference between a good player and a very good player.

Sometimes players do not combine a second chance with the first simply because they do not spot the second chance. Test yourself here:

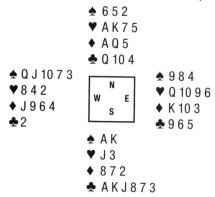

West leads the ♠Q against your small slam in clubs. How will you play?

The original declarer noted the two potential losers in diamonds and reckoned that a finesse of dummy's queen was the only chance. He did not think much of his luck when the finesse failed and he went down one. Did you spot any other chance on the deal?

If East holds the queen of hearts, you can set up a third heart trick by leading towards your ♥J. Win the spade lead and draw trumps in three rounds, ending in the dummy. Now lead a low heart towards the jack. When East holds the ♥Q you will make the contract. If he rises with the card, you will cash the ♥J later and throw two diamonds on the heart ace-king (using the ♦A as an entry). If instead East plays low, the ♥J will win and you will throw one diamond on dummy's top hearts, losing just one diamond.

If you are unlucky and the jack of hearts loses to the queen with West, you will still be able to take the diamond finesse. Once again, two chances (♥Q with East or ♦K with West) are better than one.

Do you see why you have to play hearts before diamonds? If you take a losing diamond finesse first, the queen of hearts will be a second trick for the defense, even when it is well placed (with East). By playing hearts first, you combine the two chances.

Summary

✓ There is no need to be a mathematical whiz-kid to work out the best line of play. It is a sound general guideline that two chances are better than one. Try to combine two options rather than relying on just one.

✓ When a losing trump finesse will be fatal, consider playing for the drop in trumps, hoping to obtain discards if this fails.

✓ When you have a choice of finesses for the contract but the defenders will cash enough tricks to beat you if a finesse fails, play for the drop in the longer suit before finessing in the other.

COMBINING TWO CHANCES

NOW TRY THESE...

1)

♠ 9 7
♥ J 6 5 2
♦ Q J 10 6
♣ K Q 4

```
      N
   W     E
      S
```

♠ A 6
♥ A K 8
♦ A 9 7 3
♣ A J 9 3

West leads the ♠K against 3NT. Plan the play.

2)

♠ Q 9 3
♥ A J 9 6
♦ J 7 6 2
♣ A 5

```
      N
   W     E
      S
```

♠ A K J 10 8 4
♥ Q 10 4
♦ A K
♣ 9 3

West leads the ♣K against your small slam in spades. Plan the play.

3)

♠ A 8 4
♥ A J 10 3
♦ K J 10 5
♣ A 2

```
      N
   W     E
      S
```

♠ 7 5
♥ Q 6
♦ A 7 3
♣ K Q J 10 7 4

West leads the ♠Q against six clubs. Plan the play.

ANSWERS

1) You can count eight top tricks and a successful diamond finesse will carry you past the finishing post. If it fails, of course, the defenders will cash enough spade tricks to beat the contract. There is no need to rely on this chance alone. Before taking the diamond finesse, you should play the ace and king of hearts. If the ♥Q falls in two rounds, dummy's ♥J will bring you a ninth trick without having to risk the diamond finesse.

   Note that it would not be a good idea to play four rounds of clubs first (in the misguided hope that a defender may discard a heart from Q-x-x). If the queen of hearts does not fall in two rounds, you will need to cross to dummy to take the diamond finesse. If you have already played four rounds of clubs, there will be no entry to dummy.

2) You have a potential loser in both clubs and hearts. If the heart finesse is right, you will avoid both these losers, since you can then throw a club on the fourth round of hearts. There is no need to rely solely on this chance. Win the club lead and draw two rounds of trumps with the ace and king. After playing the ace and king of diamonds, cross to dummy with the queen of trumps and ruff a diamond. If a defender started with Q-x-x, Q-x or singleton queen in the diamond suit, dummy's jack of diamonds will be good for a discard of the losing club. (You will cross to the ace of hearts to take the discard, spurning the heart finesse.) Playing to drop the diamond queen is a substantial extra chance. If it fails, nothing has been lost; you can still take the heart finesse anyway.

3) The opening lead has exposed a loser in spades. Win with the spade ace and draw trumps. If West holds the ♥K, you can make the contract by running the ♥Q. (Whether or not West covers, you will be able to throw your spade loser on the third round of the suit.) Similarly, you can make the contract by taking a successful finesse of the ♦J. If it wins, you will return to the diamond ace to finesse the ♦10. You can then throw your spade loser on the fourth round of diamonds. Which finesse should you take?

   Rather than relying solely on one of these finesses, you should combine two chances by first playing for the drop in diamonds. If the ♦Q falls in two rounds, you will discard the spade loser. (You can then return to your hand with a spade ruff to take the heart finesse for an overtrick.) If the ♦Q does not drop in two rounds, you will need to take the heart finesse. You must therefore test diamonds by playing the king first and then the ace. This will leave you in the South hand, ready for a heart finesse.

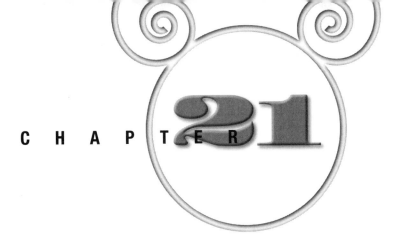

C H A P T E R 21

KEEPING THE DANGER HAND OFF LEAD

 If the leader has a card of re-entry, you cannot prevent him bringing in his suit, but you can finesse against him and make it difficult for him unless he holds an ace.
W. Dalton. *Practical Bridge. 1908*

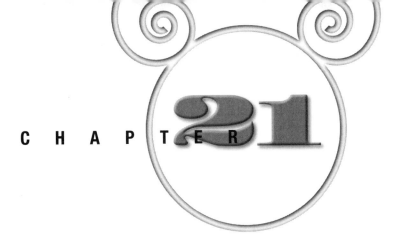

Sometimes you say to yourself: 'I could be in trouble if East gains the lead. He'll lead through my king of clubs.' In such a situation you must try to develop the tricks you need without allowing East, the dangerous defender, on lead. We have seen in previous chapters some of the ways you can achieve this — by finessing into the safe hand, for example. It's an important topic, and in this chapter we will look at some further clever moves that are at your disposal.

The key play often comes as early as the first trick. That's the case here:

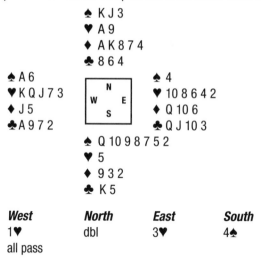

♠ K J 3
♥ A 9
♦ A K 8 7 4
♣ 8 6 4

♠ A 6
♥ K Q J 7 3
♦ J 5
♣ A 9 7 2

♠ 4
♥ 10 8 6 4 2
♦ Q 10 6
♣ Q J 10 3

♠ Q 10 9 8 7 5 2
♥ 5
♦ 9 3 2
♣ K 5

West	North	East	South
1♥	dbl	3♥	4♠
all pass			

West leads the king of hearts against 4♠. What is your plan?

You have one certain loser in spades and another in diamonds. The ace of clubs is likely to lie with West, so to avoid losing two club tricks as well you must set up dummy's diamond suit. Suppose you win the heart lead and draw trumps. When you set up the diamonds, East (who holds three diamonds) will gain the lead. A club switch through your king will beat the contract. What else can you try?

There is only one way to make the contract and that is to duck the king of hearts opening lead! Do you see why? The safe hand (West) will be left on play and you will subsequently be able to throw a diamond on the ace of hearts. That will allow you to set up the diamonds, by ruffing one round, without allowing East on lead.

How does the play go? You duck the heart lead and win the heart continuation with the ace, throwing a diamond from your hand. When you turn to the trump suit, West will win the first or second round with the ace. There is nothing he can do. If he plays ace and another club, your king will score. If instead he exits safely in diamonds (or with a second round of trumps), you will draw any outstanding trump and play the two top diamonds, pleased to see a 3-2 break. You can then ruff a diamond, to set up the suit, and return to dummy with a third round of trumps to discard both your club losers on the established long cards in diamonds.

When your left-hand opponent is the danger hand it may pay you to duck the opening lead to his partner, even when you have no loser in the suit led. Look at this deal:

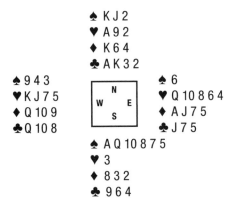

```
              ♠ K J 2
              ♥ A 9 2
              ♦ K 6 4
              ♣ A K 3 2
♠ 9 4 3                      ♠ 6
♥ K J 7 5                    ♥ Q 10 8 6 4
♦ Q 10 9                     ♦ A J 7 5
♣ Q 10 8                     ♣ J 7 5
              ♠ A Q 10 8 7 5
              ♥ 3
              ♦ 8 3 2
              ♣ 9 6 4
```

You open a weak 2♠ on the South hand and North raises you to 4♠. (3NT would have been easier.) How will you play the spade game when West leads the ♥5?

You have a certain loser in clubs, so you must avoid losing three further tricks in the diamond suit. You may well have to lead towards the diamond king at some stage, hoping that West holds the ace. Before that, there is a chance of finding the clubs 3-3 and setting up a discard.

Suppose you win the heart lead, draw two rounds of trumps and play ace, king and another club. The suit will break 3-3 all right, but West will win the third round. A diamond switch through the king will then beat the contract. Nor is there much chance of ducking an early round of clubs to East. If you lead the ♣9 with this intention, West will surely cover with the ten.

Let's try some magic on the first trick, playing dummy's nine of hearts instead of the ace! East, the safe hand, will win the trick. You can then win his heart return with the ace, throwing a club from your hand. You draw two rounds of trumps with the king and ace. Next you play the ace and king of clubs and ruff a club with the queen. When the suit breaks 3-3, you cross to dummy with a third round of trumps and discard one of your diamond losers on the thirteenth club. With the contract secure, you can ruff a heart back to your hand and seek an overtrick by leading towards the king of diamonds.

Way back in Chapter 1 (remember?) we discussed the merits of leading towards honor cards. When you need to keep a particular defender off lead, it can even be worthwhile to lead towards an ace-king combination. That's the case on this deal:

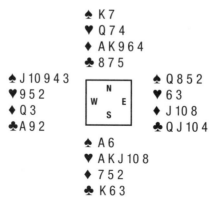

```
                      ♠ K 7
                      ♥ Q 7 4
                      ♦ A K 9 6 4
                      ♣ 8 7 5
     ♠ J 10 9 4 3                    ♠ Q 8 5 2
     ♥ 9 5 2          N              ♥ 6 3
     ♦ Q 3        W       E          ♦ J 10 8
     ♣ A 9 2          S              ♣ Q J 10 4
                      ♠ A 6
                      ♥ A K J 10 8
                      ♦ 7 5 2
                      ♣ K 6 3
```

West leads the spade jack against your game in hearts. You have a certain diamond loser and must avoid three club losers to go with it. You would like to set up the diamonds but if East gains the lead a club switch through your king will put your contract at risk. What is the best plan?

You should win the spade lead with the ace, retaining the king as a later entry to dummy. Suppose you draw trumps in three rounds and continue with ace, king and another diamond. All would be well if West had started with three diamonds, since the safe hand would win the third round. As the cards lie in our diagram, East will win. A club switch will then beat the contract.

You can set up the diamond suit safely when West holds either three diamonds or a doubleton queen. After drawing just two rounds of trumps with the ace and jack, lead a low diamond towards dummy. If West plays the queen, you will duck (leaving the safe hand on lead) and the suit will then be ready to run. West will probably play low instead, in which case you will win with dummy's ace. You return to your hand with a third round of trumps and lead a low diamond towards dummy's king. This time the queen does appear and you duck the trick. With West on lead, the defenders pose no threat. The remainder of the diamond suit is now good and you will be able to discard two of your club losers.

Suppose the cards lay differently and West did not produce the queen on the second round. You would win with dummy's king and play a third diamond, hoping that West won the trick. Dummy's king of spades would serve as an entry to the long diamonds.

BY THE WAY

You could employ the same technique with ♦A-K-9-4 in dummy and ♦7-5-2 in your hand. Hoping for a 3-3 break and needing to keep East off play, you would lead twice towards the honors in dummy.

We will end the chapter with something a little bit different. You finesse into the safe hand to guard against a bad break in a suit. Would you have played this deal correctly?

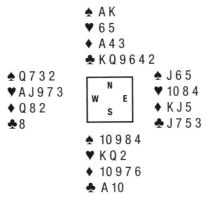

♠ A K
♥ 6 5
♦ A 4 3
♣ K Q 9 6 4 2

♠ Q 7 3 2
♥ A J 9 7 3
♦ Q 8 2
♣ 8

♠ J 6 5
♥ 10 8 4
♦ K J 5
♣ J 7 5 3

♠ 10 9 8 4
♥ K Q 2
♦ 10 9 7 6
♣ A 10

West leads the ♥7 against 3NT and you win East's ♥10 with the queen. What now?

You have seven top tricks and the club suit may provide several more. Suppose you continue with the ace of clubs and the ten of clubs to dummy's king. Ouch! West shows out on the second round and you will not be able to set up the club suit without allowing East on lead. A heart through your king will then spell defeat.

Since a full six club tricks are not needed for the contract, you don't mind losing a trick in the suit — so long as it is lost to the safe (West) hand, who cannot play a second round of hearts profitably. At Trick 2 you should cross to dummy with a spade. You then play a club and finesse the ten. You don't mind in the least if West wins with the jack. He can do no damage from his side of the table and when you regain the lead you will score five club tricks, to bring your total to nine. As the cards lie, of course, the ♦10 will win. You will bring in the whole club suit and end with ten tricks.

BY THE WAY

You could attempt the same play with only ♣A-8 in your hand. If East holds ♣J-7-5-3 or ♣10-7-5-3, he will be powerless to stop you finessing the ♣8 into the safe West hand. If instead East holds ♣J-10-5-3, he can prevent the play by rising with the jack or ten. Perhaps he will be half asleep and play a low card anyway. Then a finesse of the ♣8 will win and you will have a story to tell afterwards!

Summary

✓ When your left-hand opponent chooses a high honor as his opening lead (for example a king, when you hold the ace) it can sometimes be beneficial to duck, even in a suit contract. By doing so, you may prevent the other defender — the danger hand — from gaining the lead.

✓ Similarly, when the opening lead is a low card it may be beneficial to duck the trick to your right-hand opponent. This may prevent the opening leader from gaining the lead later in the play.

✓ When you are attempting to set up a suit such as A-K-x-x-x in dummy opposite x-x-x in your hand, you can sometimes keep your right-hand opponent off lead by leading twice towards dummy's honors. You plan to duck if the queen appears on your left.

KEEPING THE DANGER HAND OFF LEAD

NOW TRY THESE...

1)

        ♠ 9 8 3
        ♥ A 6
        ♦ A Q J 6 3
        ♣ 6 5 2

        ♠ A Q J 10 6
        ♥ 7 4
        ♦ K 10 4 2
        ♣ K 7

West leads the ♥K against your game in spades. Plan the play.

2)

        ♠ J 10 5 4
        ♥ A 7
        ♦ Q 8 5
        ♣ Q J 10 4

        ♠ K Q 9 8 6
        ♥ 10 3
        ♦ 7 4 3
        ♣ A K 3

East deals and opens the bidding 1♥, West eventually leading the ♥2 against your partscore of three spades. Plan the play.

3)

        ♠ 8 3
        ♥ K 6 3
        ♦ 10 7 3
        ♣ A K 7 6 2

        ♠ K Q 4
        ♥ A 10 4 2
        ♦ A K 2
        ♣ 9 5 3

West leads the ♠5 against 3NT, East playing the ten. Plan the play.

ANSWERS

1) Suppose you win the opening lead with dummy's ace and take a trump finesse, which loses. West will have the opportunity to cross to his partner's hand in the heart suit (by underleading his queen-jack, for example, so that East can win with the ten). A club switch will then put the contract at risk. To prevent any chance of East gaining the lead, you should duck the opening lead. You win the heart continuation and take the trump finesse. If West wins he will not be able to reach his partner's hand. Whatever he returns, you will draw the remaining trumps and discard two clubs on dummy's diamond suit.

2) You have two losers in the majors and would like to avoid losing three more tricks in diamonds. Suppose you win the opening heart lead and play a trump. If East wins the trick he will be able to cross to his partner's hand in hearts. You may then lose three diamond tricks even when East holds ♦A-K-J-x or ♦A-K-10-x and could not play the suit successfully from his side of the table.

   Since you do not want West to regain the lead and play a diamond through the queen, you should play low at Trick 1. (If West holds the ace or king of diamonds and the defenders take three diamond tricks at this stage, you could not have avoided defeat anyway.) Win the heart return and play a trump. If East wins with the ace, and also holds the diamond ace and king, he will not be able to reach his partner's hand. You will eventually throw a diamond on dummy's fourth club.

3) You win the first round of spades and observe that East is now the danger hand. If he gains the lead he will be able to lead a spade through your remaining honor in the suit. You must therefore aim to set up dummy's clubs without allowing East on lead. This will be easy enough if West holds three clubs to East's two, since West will have to win the third round. You can succeed also when West holds Q-x of clubs, provided you lead twice towards dummy's ace-king. Lead a club at Trick 2. If the queen appears from West, allow it to hold. Otherwise win with dummy's ace of clubs and return to your hand with a diamond or a heart to lead a second round of clubs. Duck if the queen appears from West. Otherwise play ace and another club, hoping that West holds three clubs and wins the trick.

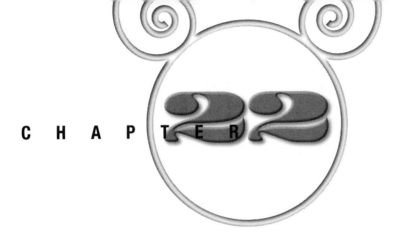

C H A P T E R 22

PLAYING A CONTRACT SAFELY

 Do not be careless; make sure of your contract if there is the slightest risk to it. **W. Dalton.** *Practical Bridge. 1908*

Back in Chapter 7 we looked at safety plays within a single suit — how you could give yourself the maximum chance of scoring the number of tricks that you needed. Now we widen the field and look at ways in which you can give yourself the best chance of making your contract. Again you will be willing to surrender the possible chance of overtricks in search of those valuable prizes — the game bonus and the slam bonus.

Let's start with a fairly ordinary-looking 3NT contract.

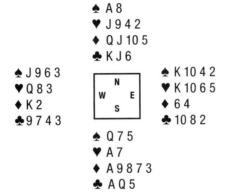

♠ A 8
♥ J 9 4 2
♦ Q J 10 5
♣ K J 6

♠ J 9 6 3   ♠ K 10 4 2
♥ Q 8 3   ♥ K 10 6 5
♦ K 2   ♦ 6 4
♣ 9 7 4 3   ♣ 10 8 2

♠ Q 7 5
♥ A 7
♦ A 9 8 7 3
♣ A Q 5

West leads the ♠3 against 3NT. What is your plan?

Suppose you play low from dummy and East wins with the king. You win the
♠2 return with dummy's ace and run the queen of diamonds, losing to the king.
West clears the spade suit and you score ten tricks. What was the point of that
hand, you may be wondering.

It was not a safe way to play the contract! What if East had concluded that
his side would need a trick or two outside the spade suit to beat the contract and
had switched to a heart at Trick 2? You would have gone down. West would win
the first round of hearts with the queen and return the ♥8 to the stiff ace. When
the diamond finesse lost, the defenders would score two more heart tricks to
defeat the game.

Once you foresee what might happen, it is easy enough to avoid any such
risk. You rise with dummy's ace of spades at Trick 1 and run the queen of diamonds. The finesse loses but the contract is guaranteed. However the spades
divide, West cannot pursue spades profitably from his side of the table. You will
win his return and make nine tricks.

That was a typical safety play. You gave up a possible overtrick (if West had
led from the king of spades) in exchange for guaranteeing your contract. The
next deal illustrates another type of safety play. You don't guarantee the contract
this time, but you give yourself an extra chance of making it.

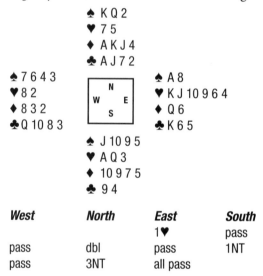

♠ K Q 2
♥ 7 5
♦ A K J 4
♣ A J 7 2

♠ 7 6 4 3
♥ 8 2
♦ 8 3 2
♣ Q 10 8 3

♠ A 8
♥ K J 10 9 6 4
♦ Q 6
♣ K 6 5

♠ J 10 9 5
♥ A Q 3
♦ 10 9 7 5
♣ 9 4

West	North	East	South
		1♥	pass
pass	dbl	pass	1NT
pass	3NT	all pass	

West leads the ♥8 and East overtakes with the nine. You win with the queen
and play a spade to the king and ace. When East persists with the king of hearts,
you duck for one round (this is safe, because there is no switch that you fear). He
plays a third round of hearts to your ace and West discards a spade. What now?

You can count eight top tricks at this stage. One extra trick from the diamond suit will therefore give you your game. In isolation, the best play in the
diamond suit — missing five cards to the queen — is to play the ace first (in case
East has a singleton queen) and then to finesse on the second round. The dia-

mond finesse is into the danger hand, however. If it fails, East will cash enough hearts to beat you. Since you need only one extra diamond trick and not two, you should make the safety play of cashing both the ace and king of diamonds. The gain comes when the cards lie as in the diagram. The doubleton queen falls from East and you make a game that would otherwise have gone down.

What if the ♦Q does not fall and West started with either ♦Q-x-x or ♦Q-x-x-x? You simply force out the diamond queen, setting up the one extra diamond trick that you need. West has already shown out of hearts, so he can do you no damage. All you will have lost is a potential overtrick.

Safety play to maintain an entry

Let's look now at a deal where a lack of entries to dummy forces you to take a safety play in the suit you are developing.

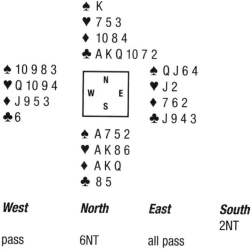

♠ K
♥ 7 5 3
♦ 10 8 4
♣ A K Q 10 7 2

♠ 10 9 8 3
♥ Q 10 9 4
♦ J 9 5 3
♣ 6

♠ Q J 6 4
♥ J 2
♦ 7 6 2
♣ J 9 4 3

♠ A 7 5 2
♥ A K 8 6
♦ A K Q
♣ 8 5

West	North	East	South
			2NT
pass	6NT	all pass	

West leads the ♠10 against your contract of 6NT. It's an annoying lead because it removes an entry to dummy's clubs. Suppose you play the ace and king of clubs next, West showing out on the second round. What can you do?

That's an easy one to answer. Nothing! Let's start again, this time with the recommended first step in any contract — making a plan. There are ten top tricks, so you need two more. In other words, five club tricks will be enough for the contract. You do not need all six.

One possibility is to lead a low club from dummy at Trick 2. Since you will still have a club in your hand when you regain the lead, the remaining clubs will be ready to run. Another line of play is possible. You cross to your hand with a diamond at Trick 2 and finesse the ten of clubs. Again you would make twelve tricks as the cards lie. The reason why you might consider this line is that you would still make an overtrick if West held J, J-x, J-x-x or J-x-x-x of clubs. What do you think of that?

The only problem with finessing the ten of clubs (a tiny one) is that you would go down when West held all five clubs! The finesse would win but you would make only four club tricks. However, by playing a low club from both hands on the first round, you would see in good time that East was void in the suit. You could then finesse dummy's ten on the second round. (If East started with all five clubs, there is nothing you can do about it.)

Discovery play

In Chapter 7 we saw that the best play in a suit often depends on the number of tricks you need from it. Sometimes you can discover how many tricks you need from a suit only by playing first on a different suit. If it lies poorly, you will need the maximum number of tricks from the first suit. If it lies well, you will need a trick fewer from the first suit and can employ a safety play. It's a difficult concept but a sample deal should make it clear.

```
              ♠ A K J 4
              ♥ K 7
              ♦ Q 8 3
              ♣ A 9 5 2
♠ 10 9 7 3                    ♠ Q 6
♥ Q J 10 3         N          ♥ 9 8 5 4 2
♦ K 9 6       W       E       ♦ A 10 4
♣ K 7             S           ♣ 8 6 3
              ♠ 8 5 2
              ♥ A 6
              ♦ J 7 5 2
              ♣ Q J 10 4
```

BY THE WAY

The early play in the club suit on this deal is known as a 'discovery play'. By discovering the lie of one suit, you determine how to play another.

West leads the ♥Q against 3NT and you note that there is a safety play available in spades. To give yourself the best chance of three spade tricks, you should cash the ace and king first (gaining when East holds ♠Q-x). If the queen does not drop, you will lead towards the ♠J on the third round, still making the required three tricks when West holds the spade queen or when the suit breaks 3-3.

Can you afford to take this safety play in spades? You don't know until you have taken the club finesse! Win the heart lead and run the queen of clubs. If the finesse succeeds, you will repeat it until you discover the lie of the club suit. Here West holds the ♣K. You therefore have a total of six top tricks outside the spade suit. With only three spade tricks needed, you can afford to employ the safety play. If instead East had held the ♣K, you would need four tricks from the spade suit. You would finesse the spade jack, hoping to find West with Q-x-x.

Safety plays in the trump suit when you need to take ruffs

When the safety of the contract is your prime concern, you may have to play the trump suit in an unusual way. In particular, you will often have to spurn the 'eight ever, nine never' guideline, to ensure that you can take the ruffs that you need. This is a typical such deal:

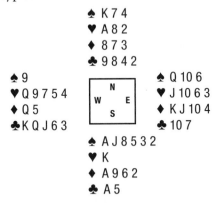

West leads the ♣K against your game in spades. How will you play?

You win with the ♣A and unblock the ♥K, preparing for a discard. You then cross to the trump king and throw a club on the ♥A. What now?

Missing four trumps to the queen, you would normally play for the drop. That would lead to defeat here. Not only would you lose a trump trick to East's queen, you would also lose three diamond tricks. (When East gained the lead in the diamond suit he would draw dummy's last trump.) The safety play is to finesse the jack of trumps when East follows suit on the second round. You don't mind at all if you lose to a doubleton queen with West. You will then have a spare trump in dummy if you need to ruff the fourth round of diamonds.

BY THE WAY

Finessing in the trump suit would be the right play even at matchpoints. When you are missing four cards to the queen, the odds in favor of playing for the drop (rather than finessing) are very slight. It is well worth flouting them when this will protect you against a 4-2 break in diamonds.

On the next deal you must ignore the 'eight ever' part of the guideline.

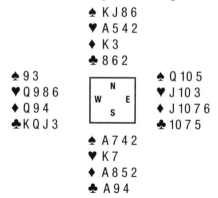

♠ K J 8 6
♥ A 5 4 2
♦ K 3
♣ 8 6 2

♠ 9 3
♥ Q 9 8 6
♦ Q 9 4
♣ K Q J 3

♠ Q 10 5
♥ J 10 3
♦ J 10 7 6
♣ 10 7 5

♠ A 7 4 2
♥ K 7
♦ A 8 5 2
♣ A 9 4

Playing in four spades, you win the ♣K lead with the ace. Suppose you make the 'normal' play in the trump suit next, cashing the ace and finessing dummy's jack. If East wins with the queen and returns another trump, you will go down. There will be only one trump left in dummy and you have two diamond losers to ruff.

The safest way to play the hand is to play the ace and king of trumps. You can then ruff two diamonds in the dummy and two hearts in your hand, not caring when the defenders score their queen of trumps.

Summary

✓ The 'normal' play in a suit may not be best when you are trying to maximize the safety of a contract.

✓ The 'eight ever, nine never' rule is a general guideline only. Always consider what will happen if your chosen play fails.

PLAYING A CONTRACT SAFELY

NOW TRY THESE...

1)

     ♠ 9 3
     ♥ A J 10
     ♦ Q J 6 3
     ♣ A J 9 4

```
        N
     W     E
        S
```

     ♠ A 8 6
     ♥ 7 5
     ♦ A 10 9 5 2
     ♣ K 10 6

West, who opened 3♠, leads the king of spades against 3NT. Plan the play.

2)

     ♠ 5 3
     ♥ A K 6
     ♦ J 9 6 3
     ♣ K 8 6 4

```
        N
     W     E
        S
```

     ♠ K Q 6
     ♥ 10 3
     ♦ A K 8 5 2
     ♣ A 5 3

West leads the ♣4 against 3NT, East playing the jack. Plan the play.

3)

     ♠ A 10 3
     ♥ K 7 2
     ♦ A 10
     ♣ A K 7 6 4

```
        N
     W     E
        S
```

     ♠ K J 9 7 6 2
     ♥ 8 5 3
     ♦ 6
     ♣ Q J 5

West leads the ♦K against four spades. Plan the play.

ANSWERS

1) You should duck the first spade, to ensure that you break the East-West communications even if West has opened on a six-card suit. Win the next spade and aim to score nine tricks without letting West on lead. Four diamonds, three clubs and two major-suit aces will be sufficient. You should not take a diamond finesse, because this would risk West gaining the lead with a singleton ♦K. Instead, play ace and another diamond. If West started with ♦K-x there was nothing you could do. If instead East wins the trick, your general plan is to set up a ninth trick by taking a club finesse into the safe (East) hand. If East started with ♦K-x, he will have to help you by playing a heart or a club. Should he exit with a heart honor, you must let it win (just in case West has the other missing honor).

    The only other possibility is that West switches to a heart at Trick 2. You will then have to finesse. If East wins and is able to clear the spades, play as before. No other return from East will threaten the contract.

2) You need four diamond tricks to bring your total to nine. The normal play in the suit, aiming for at least four tricks, would be to cash the ace first. If either defender showed out, you could then guarantee four diamond tricks by leading low towards the dummy. That is not the best line in the context of this contract because you would lose a trick to East (the danger hand) when he started with Q-10-x or Q-10-x-x. Instead you should cross to dummy with a heart (or a club) and lead a low diamond. If East plays the four or the seven, cover with the five or eight respectively. If West wins the trick, the rest of the diamond suit will be yours. If instead West shows out, return to dummy and take further finesses against East.

    If East inserts the queen or ten on the first round of diamonds, win and cross back to dummy to take further diamond finesses. Even if East started with Q-10-7-4, he cannot gain the lead.

    If East shows out on the first round of diamonds, rise with the ace and lead low towards dummy, restricting West to one diamond trick.

3) After winning the diamond lead, you must decide how to play the trump suit. Suppose you play the ace and king of trumps and find that West started with Q-x-x in the suit. Your contract is now at risk. When you turn to the club suit, West may ruff and lead a heart through dummy's king. To prevent this from happening, you should run the ♠J into the safe East hand at Trick 2. If the finesse loses, East cannot attack hearts successfully from his side of the table. You are almost certain to make an overtrick.

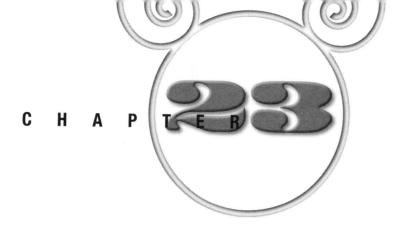

C H A P T E R 23

COUNTING THE
DEFENDERS' SHAPE

> Players do not watch the fall of the small cards closely; every teacher of the game tells one that one ought to do so, but practically, one does not. **W. Dalton.** *Practical Bridge. 1908*

You cannot become a top-class declarer unless you are willing to put some hard work into your card play. (You're tempted to throw the book out of the window? Hold on a minute.) The most important aspect of this is being willing to 'count the hand'. What does that mean? It means keeping track of what cards have gone and determining the shape of the defenders' hands.

It is not as difficult as you might think. The first piece of information may come from the opening lead. Suppose you are playing in four spades and this is the diamond position:

```
                      ♦ A 5
                      ┌─────┐
                      │  N  │
        ♦ 2 led       │W   E│      ♦ ?
                      │  S  │
                      └─────┘
                      ♦ K 10
```

If West is playing standard fourth-best opening leads, you can tell immediately that West holds four diamonds and East has five. Perhaps you draw trumps next, which will tell you the lie of that suit. You are half-way to a complete count of the defenders' shape. Play one more suit, watching for a defender to show out, and the task will be completed.

What is the benefit of all this hard work, you may be wondering. One advantage is that it can help you to guess a two-way finesse correctly. Look at this deal:

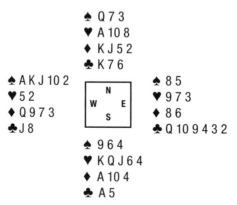

```
              ♠ Q 7 3
              ♥ A 10 8
              ♦ K J 5 2
              ♣ K 7 6
♠ A K J 10 2              ♠ 8 5
♥ 5 2          N          ♥ 9 7 3
♦ Q 9 7 3    W   E        ♦ 8 6
♣ J 8          S          ♣ Q 10 9 4 3 2
              ♠ 9 6 4
              ♥ K Q J 6 4
              ♦ A 10 4
              ♣ A 5
```

You open 1♥ on the South cards and West overcalls 1♠. He subsequently leads the two top spades against your heart game and gives his partner a spade ruff. Back comes a trump and you draw trumps in one more round. You have a two-way finessing position in diamonds and must guess who holds the diamond queen in order to make the contract. Any ideas?

If you had to guess immediately, you would play East for the missing queen. That's because he has shown up with five cards in the majors to his partner's seven. He therefore has eight vacant places in his hand to accommodate diamonds, whereas West has only six. It costs nothing to have a look at the club situation, though. You play the ace and king of clubs and ruff a third round. West shows out and the picture changes! You now know that West's shape is 5-2-4-2. Since he holds four diamonds to his partner's two, he is twice as likely as East to hold the diamond queen. You play the diamond ace and finesse dummy's jack. Justice is served on this occasion and you make your game.

If West had followed to the third club, you would know that East held at least three diamonds and maybe more. You would be inclined to finesse East for the queen of diamonds.

When an opponent preempts, or makes a two-suited overcall, it is usually quite easy for declarer to obtain a count on his hand. Test yourself on this deal:

1)

♠ Q 7 4
♥ A Q 6
♦ K 10 7
♣ K 8 7 2

♠ A K J 10 9
♥ K 9 4
♦ A J 2
♣ A 5

West leads a trump against your grand slam in spades. Plan the contract.

2)

♠ K J 7 5 2
♥ 8 6
♦ Q 9 2
♣ A K 3

♠ A Q 8 6 3
♥ A J
♦ A K 7
♣ J 6 4

East opens 3♥ and you bid to a small slam in spades. How will you play the contract when West leads the ♥9 and East plays the queen?

3)

♠ A 5 2
♥ A Q 9
♦ K Q 10 4
♣ K 8 3

♠ K Q 3
♥ K 8 4
♦ A 9 5 2
♣ A 5 4

West leads the ♠J against 6NT. How will you play the contract?

ANSWERS

1) The contract depends on your guess in the diamond suit, where you have a two-way finesse. To maximize your chances, you should aim for a complete count on the hand (or as good a count as you can get).

Suppose you draw trumps, finding East with three. You next play the ace and king of clubs and ruff a club, both defenders following. When you cross to dummy with a heart and lead the last club, it is East who follows. You ruff with your last trump and play two more rounds of hearts, both defenders following all the way. You don't know where the last heart is but you do know that East's shape is either 3-3-3-4 or 3-4-2-4. So, West has four or five diamonds; East has two or three. That makes West a clear favorite to hold the diamond queen and you should finesse him for that card.

If one of the defenders had shown out on the third round of hearts, you would have had a complete count on the hand. As we just saw, though, you can still greatly improve your chances even when you do not have a complete count.

2) The correct line of play will depend on a complete count of the hand. You can assume from East's opening bid, and the lead, that hearts are divided 2-7. Suppose you win East's queen of hearts with the ace and draw trumps, finding that East has just one trump. You then play the three diamond winners, East showing out on the third round. You know at this stage that East's count is 1-7-2-3. You will put East on lead with a heart. He will then have to play a club (or give you a ruff-and-sluff). You must hope that he is leading from the ♣Q. Your ♣J will then win.

Suppose instead that East followed to one trump and all three diamonds. You would know that he could hold at most two clubs. You would play the ace and king of clubs before putting East on lead with a heart. He would then have to give you a ruff-and-sluff.

3) You have eleven top tricks and will score a twelfth from the diamond suit unless one defender holds ♦J-x-x-x and you misguess which defender that is. (If you play the ace and king of diamonds first, you will fail when East holds ♦J-x-x-x; if you play the king and queen, you fail when West holds ♦J-x-x-x.) Win the spade lead and duck a club. You can then play three rounds of each suit outside diamonds, aiming for a complete count before making your diamond guess. If West shows five spades, for example, and follows to three hearts and two clubs, he cannot hold four diamonds as well. You will therefore play the king and queen of diamonds first

CHAPTER 24

COUNTING THE DEFENDERS' POINTS

 Note carefully the card that is led, and try to make out what it has been led from, which ought not to be a difficult task when you can see twenty-seven cards. **W. Dalton.** *Practical Bridge. 1908*

Do you enjoy counting? No, it's not very high on our list of the world's pleasures, either. It's a vital part of playing bridge well, though, and not at all difficult. The good news is that few players can be bothered to do it. If you are willing to make the effort, counting the distribution and high-card points, you can leap ahead of them!

In this chapter we will see how you can boost your card reading, as declarer, by counting the defenders' points and matching this to their action, or lack of action, during the bidding. This is a straightforward example:

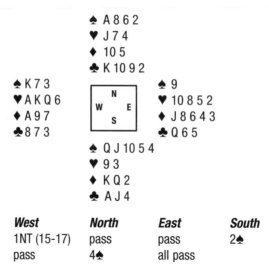

West	North	East	South
1NT (15-17)	pass	pass	2♠
pass	4♠	all pass	

You dislike the North-South bidding even more than you dislike counting? Maybe, but let's look at the play. How will you tackle the spade game when West leads the three top heart honors?

You ruff the third heart and run the queen of trumps successfully. Two more rounds of trumps clear that suit. What now? You have a certain diamond loser, so all depends on locating the ♣Q. Should you finesse West or East for the card?

The correct answer at this stage is, 'I have no idea!' In order to discover who holds the ♣Q, you must first discover where the ♦A is. When you play a diamond to the king, West wins with the ace. That gives him at least sixteen points outside clubs. If he held the ♣Q too, he would have eighteen points — too much for a 1NT opening. You therefore finesse East for the club queen, making your game. What would happen if East turned up with the ace of diamonds? West would then be marked with both the ♣Q and the ♦J to make up a minimum 15-count for his 1NT bid. You would finesse West for the club queen and once again make your contract. The actual counting may be tiresome but making your contract on both occasions is enjoyable. Admit it!

Let's dip our toes into the icy water again:

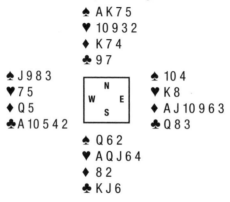

West	North	East	South
		pass	1♥
pass	3♥	pass	4♥
all pass			

West leads the ♦Q against your heart game, winning the first trick. East encourages with the jack and wins the second round of diamonds with the nine. What is your plan when East plays the ♦A at Trick 3?

You should ruff with the queen or jack, to prevent an overruff. You then cross to the spade ace and run the ten of trumps. A second round of trumps picks up the defenders' cards in the suit and leaves you with just one problem — you must guess whether to play the king or the jack on the first round of clubs. Any ideas?

East declined to open the bidding in first seat. Look at the values he has already shown: ace-jack-ten sixth in diamonds and the king of hearts. Add in the queen of clubs and some adventurous players would open 1♦, even on a 10-count. Add in the ace of clubs and *everyone* would open the bidding! Since East did not open, he cannot possibly hold the ace of clubs. After playing the queen and ace of spades, you should lead a club to the jack. This forces West's ace of clubs and the contract is yours. Your remaining club loser can be ruffed in the dummy.

Let's see one more deal where counting points and thinking back to the bidding will avoid a tricky guess.

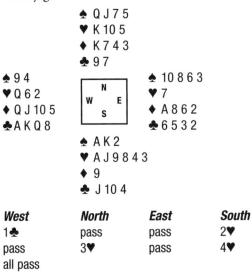

West	North	East	South
1♣	pass	pass	2♥
pass	3♥	pass	4♥
all pass			

Your jump overcall shows a fair hand after two passes. Partner gives you a single raise and you advance to game. West leads two top clubs against your heart game and switches to the queen of diamonds. How will you play the contract?

Since you have no further losers in the black suits, you might as well try the king of diamonds. East wins with the ace and returns another diamond, which you ruff. You have lost three tricks already and cannot afford a further loser in the trump suit. Any ideas?

West has shown up with twelve points already, enough for an opening bid. So, that provides no clue as to the position of the trump queen. More interesting is the fact that East has shown up with four points already (the ♦A) and failed to respond to his partner's opening bid. Since he would surely have responded with six points, you place the trump queen with West. After ruffing the second diamond, you should run the jack of trumps from your hand. Note that it would not be a good idea to cash the ace on the first round, since you could not then catch Q-x-x-x with West.

BY THE WAY

If West held ♥Q-x-x-x, it would have been good defense to play a third round of clubs, forcing dummy to ruff. You would not then have been able to pick up the queen of trumps.

Summary

✓ Counting the defenders' points will often help you to read the position of their honor cards.

✓ A player who has opened will usually hold at least twelve high-card points. A player who has failed to respond will usually hold fewer than six high-card points.

✓ When a defender has opened 1NT, you will have a close idea of his point count. When you have a key decision to make in one suit, play the other suits first, to see how many points the opener holds there.

COUNTING THE DEFENDERS' POINTS

NOW TRY THESE...

1)

♠ Q 7 3
♥ 10 6 5
♦ K 7 6
♣ J 10 7 3

```
    N
W       E
    S
```

♠ 9 6
♥ A K Q J 8 3 2
♦ A 5
♣ K 6

After three passes you open 4♥, passed out. West leads the ♠5 to East's jack. East continues with the spade ace and king. Plan the play.

2)

♠ K J 4
♥ J 6 3
♦ 10 7 2
♣ K 7 5 3

```
    N
W       E
    S
```

♠ A 10 9 7 6 2
♥ 5 4 2
♦ Q 5
♣ A 8

West opens 1NT (15-17 points) and after two passes you bid 2♠, ending the auction. West cashes the ♥A-K-Q and switches to the ♣J. Plan the play.

3)

♠ A 9 8
♥ A 9 6
♦ 7 4 2
♣ Q J 10 2

```
    N
W       E
    S
```

♠ 7
♥ K J 10 8 4 2
♦ K 8 3
♣ A K 5

West opens 1♠, followed by two passes. You are soon in 4♥ and West leads the spade queen (denying the king). How will you play the trumps?

ANSWERS

1) You can afford to ruff the third round of spades high. After drawing trumps, you will have to guess the club suit. East has already shown up with eight points (the ♠A-K-J). He cannot hold the ♣A too or he would have opened the bidding. You should therefore cross to dummy's king of diamonds and run the jack of clubs, hoping that East holds the queen. Some chance is better than none!

2) If West held the ace and king of diamonds he would surely have switched to that suit at Trick 4. So, you can place West with only one diamond honor. The jack of clubs switch suggests that East holds the queen of that suit. If West's honors outside the trump suit are indee ♥A-K-Q, ♦A or ♦K, ♣J, he must have the queen of trumps to make up his fifteen-count. The evidence you have seen strongly suggests that you should finesse West for the trump queen.

3) East failed to respond to 1♠. He is already marked with the spade king and might hold a diamond honor such as the jack. The queen of trumps in addition would then give him enough to respond to his partner's bid. If your contract depended on guessing the position of the queen of trumps, you would finesse West for the card.

Whenever you are considering a play in one suit, you must always check that your intended play makes sense in terms of giving yourself the best chance to make the contract. Suppose you run the jack of trumps and East wins, beating your contract with a diamond switch. Your complaints that West had opened on a mere 10-count are unlikely to impress your partner! Even though West is a strong favorite to hold the trump queen, the contract is cold if you finesse East for that card. You don't mind losing a trump trick to West because he cannot attack diamonds. When you regain the lead you will draw trumps and throw a diamond loser on the fourth round of clubs. (Sorry if you regard this as a trick question. You have to keep your wits about you at the bridge table!)

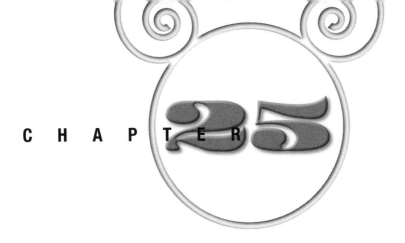

COMPARING TWO LINES OF PLAY

 One of the greatest charms of bridge is that it often offers very different methods of playing the same hand.
W. Dalton. *Practical Bridge. 1908*

Suppose you have two possible chances of making a contract. Ideally, you would like to combine them — to play for one chance and to fall back on the other, should it fail. That is not always possible and in this chapter we will look at situations where you must push your pile of chips onto a single chance. Before doing this, you will naturally want to calculate which line of play offers the best prospect.

Let's look at a typical contract that offers two different chances:

♠ Q 3
♥ K 7 5
♦ A K 10 6 4 3
♣ 8 7

♠ A K J 10 8 4
♥ A 8
♦ 7 2
♣ A Q 5

West leads the ♥J against your grand slam in spades. How would you plan the play?

You must first determine what options are available. One is to take a club finesse, ruffing the third round of clubs high if the finesse succeeds. The second is to set up the diamonds. To succeed in this second objective, you would have to win the heart lead with the ace and draw trumps. You would then play the ace-king of diamonds and ruff a diamond. If the suit broke 3-2, you could cross to the king of hearts to reach the established diamonds. Which is the better option to follow?

The club finesse is a 50% chance. You succeed when East holds the club king, fail when West has it. What is the chance of a 3-2 break? You can't work it out in your head, unless you are a mathematics professor, so you have to learn a few of the basic percentages from a book. These are the odds for the various breaks in a five-card suit:

3-2 break	*68%*
4-1 break	*28%*
5-0 break	*4%*

BY THE WAY

If you follow this line and diamonds break 4-1, it will be too late to revert to clubs. You could finesse the ♣Q, yes, but there are no trumps left in dummy, so you would not be able to ruff the third round of clubs.

As you see, a 3-2 diamond break is appreciably more likely than a successful club finesse. You should therefore win with the ace of hearts, draw trumps and try to establish the diamonds.

Here is another deal that offers two options. See what you make of it.

```
          ♠ A 7
          ♥ A J 10 6
          ♦ 9 6 5 2
          ♣ A 7 3

              ┌─────────┐
              │    N    │
              │ W     E │
              │    S    │
              └─────────┘

          ♠ K Q J 8 4 3 2
          ♥ 7 3
          ♦ A Q
          ♣ K 5
```

West leads the ♣J against your small slam in spades. You draw trumps in two rounds and play a heart to the jack, losing to the queen. When East switches to the ♦3, you have two options. Should you finesse the queen of diamonds or rise with the ace and take a second finesse in hearts, hoping that West holds the heart king?

Complete guess! many players would reply. It's 50-50 who holds the king of diamonds, 50-50 who holds the king of hearts.

Do you see the flaw in this argument? The diamond finesse is indeed a 50% chance. A second heart finesse is much better than this. Surprising as it may seem, the odds are 2-to-1 in your favor. Look at it this way. Initially there were four possible placements of the heart honors, all roughly equal in probability:

	West	*East*
A)	king and queen	no honor
B)	king	queen
C)	queen	king
D)	no honor	king and queen

In case A the first finesse will win (or West will split his honors). In cases B and C the first finesse will lose but the second will win. In case D both finesses will lose. So, 50% of the time the first finesse will lose but the second will win. Only 25% of the time will both finesses lose. It follows that once the first finesse has lost, the odds are 2-to-1 in your favor that the second will succeed. Note that it makes absolutely no difference whether East wins with the king or the queen.

You will find players who spend their entire lives disputing the logic of this. (You may have heard expert players talking about the 'Principle of Restricted Choice'. This is an example of it.) Don't be one of the doubters! East is twice as likely to hold one honor as he is to hold two. So, once the first finesse has lost, West is twice as likely as East to hold the missing honor.

Going back to the spade slam (if you haven't forgotten it by now!), the best play is to rise with the ace of diamonds and to take the second heart finesse, which will win two times out of every three.

Let's see some more deals where you must compare the chance of a favorable break with that of a finesse.

```
            ♠ K 6 3
            ♥ K 4
            ♦ A K 8 4
            ♣ J 10 6 2

            ┌─────────┐
            │    N    │
            │ W     E │
            │    S    │
            └─────────┘

            ♠ A 9 8 5 2
            ♥ 9 5 2
            ♦ Q 5 2
            ♣ A Q
```

West leads the queen of hearts against your game in spades. You play the king, in the hope that East will win with the ace and play a second heart to his partner. No, East has played the game before and he makes just the switch you did not want — a club. (This is good defense, because it forces you to decide whether to finesse in clubs before you know whether the diamonds are breaking 3-3.) Should you finesse the queen of clubs or rise with the ace, play two rounds of trumps and turn to the diamond suit?

You need a 3-2 trump break anyway. If diamonds break 3-3 as well, you will be able to throw your club loser on the fourth round. The club finesse is a 50% shot. The chance of a 3-3 diamond break is not easily calculated and you would have to look it up in a book. These are the probabilities of the various breaks when you have six cards missing:

3-3 break	*36%*
4-2 break	*48%*
5-1 break	*15%*
6-0 break	*1%*

As you see, the chance of the diamonds breaking 3-3 is appreciably less than that of a simple finesse succeeding. When East switches to a club you should therefore finesse the queen.

Those of you who did not fall asleep during your mathematics classes at school might like to consider a variation on the above deal. Give North ♦A-K-J-4 instead of ♦A-K-8-4. What would be the best line then?

Suppose you rise with the club ace and play two rounds of trumps, finding them 3-2. Again you would need to discard the ♣Q on dummy's diamonds before the defender with the last trump could ruff. The presence of the ♦J would give you a much better chance of doing this. As well as succeeding when the diamonds are 3-3, you would also make the contract when the defender with the last trump holds four or more diamonds. The total chance for the diamond play would therefore be 36% (for a 3-3 break) plus half of the 48% for a 4-2 break (only half, because the 48% covers both 4-2 and 2-4 breaks). Add in a small fraction for 5-1 and 6-0 breaks the right way and the total comes to well over 60% — much more than the 50% for the club finesse. Playing for a discard on the diamonds would then become the better line of play.

On the next deal you have seven cards missing in the suit where a favorable break is one of the chances. The other chance is a straightforward finesse in the same suit. What do you make of it?

♠ A Q 7 6 2
♥ A 9 8
♦ 6 3
♣ J 10 4

```
      N
  W       E
      S
```

♠ 5
♥ K 5 3
♦ A K 4
♣ A K Q 9 8 3

West leads a trump against your contract of 7♣. Plan the play.

You must somehow dispose of your heart loser. One option is to finesse the ♠Q — a 50% chance. If the finesse wins, you will be able to discard a heart on the ace of spades. The other option is to set up a long card in the spade suit by taking three spade ruffs in the South hand. This will succeed if the spades break 4-3. These are the odds for the various breaks when seven cards are missing:

4-3 break	*62%*
5-2 break	*30%*
6-1 break	*7%*
7-0 break	*1%*

So the chance of a 4-3 break is 62%, appreciably better than that for a finesse succeeding. You should therefore spurn the spade finesse and try to set up the thirteenth spade by ruffing in the South hand. You will succeed also when the spade king is doubleton or singleton (another 9%). How does the play go? You win the trump lead in hand, play a spade to the ace and ruff a spade high. You then cross to dummy with a trump and ruff another spade high. After cashing the two high diamonds, you reach dummy with a diamond ruff and ruff yet another spade. Finally you draw the last trump, if necessary, and return to the ace of hearts to discard a heart on the established spade.

BY THE WAY

Even if you do not hold in your mind any of the actual figures for the various breaks, remember this: an even number of outstanding cards break evenly less than half the time. An odd number of cards break as evenly as possible more than half the time.

Finally, let's look at a deal where you must compare the chances of two different breaks.

```
             ♠ 8 3
             ♥ A K 5
             ♦ A 10 8 7
             ♣ A K 8 6

              ┌─────────┐
              │    N    │
              │ W     E │
              │    S    │
              └─────────┘

             ♠ J 9 6
             ♥ 9 6 4 2
             ♦ K Q 2
             ♣ Q 7 5
```

You suppress the poor hearts and — rightly or wrongly — respond 1NT to partner's 1♣. West leads the ♠2 against the resultant 3NT contract and the defenders score four tricks in the suit. What two discards will you make from dummy?

You can spare one heart but must then throw a card from one of the minors, abandoning your chance of a ninth trick from that source. If you throw a diamond, your residual chance in clubs will be just 36%, the chance of a 3-3 break. If you make the better discard of a club, your residual chance in diamonds is more than that for a 3-3 break because you have the ♦10. You will also make the contractwhen West holds ♦J-x-x-x-x (allowing you to diagnose a finesse) and when the ♦J falls in two rounds. This gives you an extra 25% chance of making the contract!

When a robber asks you for one of your two wallets, give him (or her, of course) the smaller of the two wallets! In this case, you should hand over your chances in the club suit.

Summary

> ✓ When there is more than one chance that may give you the contract, aim to combine chances rather than rely on just one.
>
> ✓ Learn, in rough figures, the odds of the various breaks in a suit. You can then compare the chances of two different lines of play.

COMPARING TWO LINES OF PLAY

NOW TRY THESE...

1)

♠ A Q 3
♥ K 7
♦ A K 10 4
♣ Q 9 7 2

```
      N
   W     E
      S
```

♠ 8 4
♥ A Q J 10 9 6 3
♦ Q 8 3
♣ J

West leads the ♠J against your small slam in hearts. Plan the play.

2)

♠ 9 6
♥ 8 2
♦ A J 10 4
♣ A 10 8 6 2

```
      N
   W     E
      S
```

♠ A K Q J 5 4
♥ A K 5 3
♦ 7 6
♣ 3

West leads the ♥Q against your small slam in spades. Plan the play.

3)

♠ A 2
♥ 8 7 3
♦ 8 7 6 4 2
♣ A Q 3

```
      N
   W     E
      S
```

♠ K Q J 10 6 5
♥ A K Q 6
♦ K Q
♣ 8

West leads the ♣2 against your small slam in spades. Plan the play.

COMPARING TWO LINES OF PLAY

ANSWERS

1) One option is to take the spade finesse, in the hope that West holds the king of spades. The other is to rise with the spade ace, draw trumps and hope to discard your spade loser on dummy's diamond suit. What is the chance of this second option? You would succeed when diamonds were 3-3 (a 36% chance, if you look back to page 178). You would succeed also when diamonds were 4-2 and the jack fell doubleton (which is another 16% — one-third of the 48% for a 4-2 break). When West holds ♦J-x-x-x-x, East will show out on the second round and you can finesse the ♦10 (that's another 7%). Add in a small fraction for a singleton jack of diamonds and the total comes to around 61%.

   An 11% advantage in favor of relying on diamonds, then? Arithmetic is not always enough. It is not attractive to lead from a K-J-10 combination and many players would refuse to do so. In practice, the odds that the spade king is onside after a jack lead are very much less than 50%. It is therefore easily best to play for a discard on the diamonds.

2) You can see two potential heart losers and one loser in diamonds. One option is to attempt to ruff both heart losers, taking the second ruff with the nine. If the defender who has only three hearts does not hold the ten of trumps, he will not be able to overruff. What is the chance of this succeeding? Once one low heart ruff has passed by safely, which you need anyway, the chance that the ten of trumps will lie with the last heart is roughly 50%.

   The second option is to take only one heart ruff and depend on the double finesse in diamonds for an extra trick (allowing you to throw the remaining heart loser). The diamond suit will yield a second trick roughly 75% of the time — whenever East does not hold both the missing honors. So, this is the better shot. Take the first diamond finesse at Trick 2. Win the return and take just one heart ruff with the nine. After drawing trumps, you will repeat the diamond finesse, to set up a discard for your remaining heart loser.

3) You have a certain loser in diamonds and must make plans for your fourth heart. One option is to take a club finesse at Trick 1 (a 50% chance). The other option is to rise with the club ace, draw trumps, and hope that hearts break 3-3 (only 36%). You can improve slightly on the latter line by drawing just one round of trumps before playing three rounds of hearts. You will then succeed when a defender with one or two hearts holds only one trump. He will not be able to ruff and you can ruff your fourth heart in dummy. This tiny extra chance is nowhere near enough to close the 14% gap between the two lines. You should therefore take the club finesse.

GLOSSARY

Block Situation where the position of a high card, or cards, prevents the easy playing of a suit. For example, A-K opposite Q-J-3-2.

Break The division of the outstanding cards in a suit. For example you might hold eight trumps between your hand and the dummy, and the defenders' trumps break 3-2 — one of them has three, the other has two.

Cash To take a trick by leading a winning card.

Claim the contract At any stage during the play declarer is entitled to lay down his cards and claim a certain number of tricks, stating his intended line of play. The purpose of this is to save time.

Clear a suit To force out the opponents' high cards in a suit so that the remaining cards in the suit become winners.

Counting the hand Deducing the shape of the hidden hands — from bids made, cards led, and players showing out.

Cover To play a card in the suit led that is higher than that played by the previous player.

Cross To transfer the lead to the hand opposite. For example, 'He crossed to dummy with a club to the ace.'

Crossruff To score separately the trumps in declarer's hand and the dummy, by taking ruffs in alternate hands. The defenders, too, can sometimes execute a crossruff.

Danger hand The defender who will be able to make a damaging play, should he gain the lead.

Deep finesse A finesse where the opponents hold three or more cards higher in rank than the card finessed. For example, a finesse of the nine from the combination A-Q-9.

Discard To play a card (not a trump) of a different suit from the card led.

Distribution The shape of a hand (for example: 4-2-3-4, which means four spades, two hearts, three diamonds and four clubs). Also, the division of a suit among the four hands (for example, 'the clubs were distributed 4-4-4-1 round the table.')

Double finesse A finesse, often a repeated finesse, against two outstanding honor cards. (For example, with A-J-10 opposite 4-3-2, you would lead low to the jack on the first round. When the first finesse lost, you would lead low to the ten in the second round.)

Doubleton A holding of exactly two cards in a suit.

Duck To play low when you might have won the trick.

Dummy reversal A technique where declarer's hand plays the role usually associated with the dummy. Ruffs are taken in declarer's hand, rather than in the dummy.

Elimination play A technique in a suit contract, where declarer removes one or more suits from both hands and then puts a defender on lead. Since the defender cannot play an eliminated suit without giving a ruff-and-sluff, he has to play another suit — to declarer's advantage.

Entry A card that allows you to reach a particular hand.

Establish a suit To play sufficient rounds of a suit, sometimes ruffing in the other hand, sometimes conceding one or more tricks, that the remaining cards become winners.

Exit To relinquish the lead by playing a losing card.

Finesse A lead towards a card that is not a master, made in the hope that any higher card(s) will lie with the defender playing second to the trick. For example, you lead towards a king, hoping that the ace lies in front of the king.

Force To play a high card that obliges an opponent to ruff. Also, to play a high card to remove a higher card from an opponent.

Fourth-best lead Most players lead the fourth-best card from a suit that contains an honor (for example, they lead the ♥3 from ♥K-10-8-3-2).

Good A card becomes good when all higher cards have been played (for example, once the ace and king have gone, the queen is 'good').

Guard A holding that prevents the other side from running a suit. (If dummy holds A-K-x-x-x, for example, a defender's Q-J-x would guard the suit.)

High To 'play high' is to play the top card from a holding. Also, 'Dummy is high' means that all the cards in dummy are winners.

Hold up To decline to play a card that would have won the trick (for example: 'West led the king of spades and declarer held up the ace.')

Holding The cards a player has in a particular suit (for example, 'My club holding was the king and two small cards').

Honor card The ace, king, queen, jack and ten are known as honor cards. All other cards are known as spot cards.

In front of In the hand that plays before. For example, 'the ace was in front of the king' means that the player holding the ace will have to play just before the player holding the king, as here:

```
          K 4
                  ┌─────┐
                  │  N  │
    A 5           │W   E│
                  │  S  │
                  └─────┘
```

Knock out To remove a high card held by the opponents. (For example, a defender with K-Q-J might lead the king to knock out declarer's ace.)

LHO Abbreviation for left-hand opponent, the player who is sitting on your left.

Long-trump hand The hand, either dummy or declarer's, that contains more trumps than the hand opposite.

Loser A card that will lose a trick, or may lose a trick. For example, with A-6-3 in the club suit you would have two club losers.

Loser-on-loser play The act of leading a loser in one suit and discarding on it a loser from another suit. This may be tactically beneficial in various ways.

Master card A card that has become the top card in a suit, because all higher cards have already been played.

Offside Positioned so that a finesse will lose. In this diagram, the king is offside:

A Q

K 5

3 2

Onside Positioned so that a finesse will win. In this diagram, the king is onside:

A Q

K 5

3 2

Over In the hand that plays after. For example, 'the ace-queen lies over the king' means that the hand containing the king will have to play immediately before the hand containing the ace-queen, as here:

A Q

K 5

Overruff To ruff with a higher trump than that played by the opponent on your right.

Overtake To play a higher card than one already played by your side, both cards usually being honors. (For example, 'Declarer led the jack of spades from dummy and overtook with the queen.')

Promote a card To play in such a way that a particular card becomes a winner.

Reading the cards Attempting to judge where the hidden cards lie, by drawing inferences from the opponents' bidding and the cards they have played.

Return To play back the same suit. (For example, 'East won the spade lead with the ace and returned the ten of spades.')

RHO Abbreviation for right-hand opponent, the player who is sitting on your right.

Round A trick in a suit. For example, 'declarer played two rounds of trumps' means that declarer led a trump twice in succession.

Ruff To play a trump on the lead of a suit in which you are void.

Ruff-and-sluff The lead, by a defender, of a card that declarer can ruff in either hand. In practice he will ruff in one hand and discard a loser from the other. (Also known as a ruff-and-discard.)

Ruffing finesse A finesse where you lead a high card from one hand, holding a void in the other. If the card is covered, you plan to ruff; if not, you will discard a loser, hoping to win the trick with the card you led.

Run To lead a high card that is not a master, playing low from the opposite hand if the defender does not cover. Also, to 'run a suit' is to play the winners in a suit.

Safe hand The defender who cannot make a damaging play, should he gain the lead.

Safety play A play that gives you the best chance of making the contract, sometimes at the cost of surrendering the chance of an overtrick.

Second seat The player who plays second to a trick. (For example, 'South led a heart and West played low in second seat.')

Sequence Three or more honors that are consecutive, or nearly so. For example: K-Q-J or K-Q-10.

Set up a suit Alternative term for 'establish a suit'. To play a suit, sometimes ruffing and sometimes conceding a trick or two, until the remaining cards become good.

Short-trump hand The hand, either dummy or declarer's, that contains fewer trumps than the hand opposite.

Show out To fail to follow suit, having no more cards in the suit led.

Singleton A holding of just one card in a suit.

Spot card All cards from the nine down to the two are known as spot cards. The cards above the nine in rank are known as honor cards.

Stand up To win a trick because no opponent can ruff. For example, 'Three rounds of clubs stood up'.

Stopper A holding that prevents the other side from running a suit. If declarer has A-x-x in the suit led he has one 'stopper'.

Strip To remove from an opponent all his cards in a particular suit.

Switch The action taken when a player wins a trick in one suit and then leads a different suit to the next trick. For example: 'East won the the trick with the spade ace and switched to a heart.'

Tenace A combination of two cards, usually honor cards, one of which is two lower in rank than the other. (For example, an ace-queen or a king-jack.)

Third seat The player who plays third to a trick. (For example, 'West led a club, dummy played low, and East played the king in third seat.')

Throw in To put an opponent on lead, in the hope that he will make a helpful return.

Trump control Declarer is said to have lost trump control when a defender holds more trumps than he does.

Unblock To lead, follow suit with, or discard a high card that would otherwise inconvenience you (see 'Block').

Under In the hand that plays before. For example, 'the king lies under the ace-queen' means that the hand containing the king will have to play immediately before the hand containing the ace-queen, as here:

A Q

K 5

MORE BRIDGE TITLES FROM MASTER POINT PRESS

ABTA Book of the Year Award Winners

25 Bridge Conventions You Should Know
by Barbara Seagram and Marc Smith
(foreword by Eddie Kantar)
192pp., PB   Can $19.95   US $15.95

Eddie Kantar teaches Modern Bridge Defense
Eddie Kantar teaches Advanced Bridge Defense
by Eddie Kantar
each 240pp., PB   Can $27.95   US $19.95

Also available in Interactive CD-ROM Editions
Modern Bridge Defense   Can $69.95   US $49.95
Advanced Bridge Defense   Can $69.95   US $49.95

The Bridge Technique Series
by David Bird & Marc Smith
each 64pp. PB   Can $7.95   US $5.95

Deceptive Card Play	**Planning in Suit Contracts**
Defensive Signaling	**Reading the Cards**
Eliminations and Throw-Ins	**Safety Plays**
Entry Management	**Squeezes for Everyone**
Planning in Defense	**Tricks with Finesses**
Planning in Notrump Contracts	**Tricks with Trumps**

25 Bridge Myths Exposed by David Bird
200pp., PB   Can $19.95   US $15.95

Around the World in 80 Hands by Zia Mahmood with David Burn
256pp., PB   Can $22.95   US $16.95

A Study in Silver *A second collection of bridge stories* by David Silver
128pp., PB   Can $12.95   US$ 9.95

Becoming a Bridge Expert by Frank Stewart
300pp., PB   Can $27.95   US $19.95

Best of Bridge Today Digest by Matthew and Pamela Granovetter
192pp., PB   Can $19.95   US $14.95

Bridge Problems for a New Millennium by Julian Pottage
160pp., PB   Can $14.95   US $11.95

Bridge the Silver Way by David Silver and Tim Bourke
192pp., PB   Can $19.95   US $14.95

Bridge Squeezes for Everyone* **Yes, even you!* by David Bird
220pp., PB   Can $24.95   US $17.95

Bridge: 25 Steps to Learning 2/1 by Paul Thurston (foreword by Eric Kokish)
192pp., PB   Can $19.95   US $15.95

Bridge: 25 Ways to Compete in the Bidding by
Barbara Seagram and Marc Smith (foreword by Eddie Kantar)
220pp., PB   Can $19.95   US $15.95

Bridge, Zia... and me by Michael Rosenberg (foreword by Zia Mahmood)
192pp., PB   Can $19.95   US $15.95

Challenge Your Declarer Play by Danny Roth
128pp., PB   Can $12.95   US $ 9.95

Classic Kantar *a collection of bridge humor* by Eddie Kantar
192pp., PB   Can $19.95   US $14.95

Competitive Bidding in the 21st Century by Marshall Miles
254pp., PB   Can $22.95   US. $16.95

Countdown to Winning Bridge by Tim Bourke and Marc Smith
192pp., PB   Can $19.95   US $14.95

Easier Done Than Said *Brilliancy at the Bridge Table* by Prakash K. Paranjape
128pp., PB   Can $15.95   US $12.95

Eddie Kantar Teaches Topics in Declarer Play by Eddie Kantar
228pp., PB   Can $27.95   US $19.95

For Love or Money *The Life of a Bridge Journalist*
by Mark Horton and Brian Senior
189pp., PB   Can $22.95   US $16.95

Focus On Declarer Play by Danny Roth
128pp., PB   Can $12.95   US $9.95

Focus On Defence by Danny Roth
128pp., PB   Can $12.95   US $9.95

Focus On Bidding by Danny Roth
160pp., PB   Can $14.95   US $11.95

Following the LAW by Larry Cohen
176pp., PB   Can $19.95   US $15.95

How to Play Bridge with Your Spouse and Survive! by Roselyn Teukolsky
176pp., PB   Can $19.95   US $15.95

Inferences at Bridge by Marshall Miles
208pp., PB   Can $22.95   US $16.95

I Shot my Bridge Partner by Matthew Granovetter
384pp., PB   Can $19.95   US $14.95

Larry Cohen's Bidding Challenge by Larry Cohen
192pp., PB   Can $19.95   US $15.95

Murder at the Bridge Table by Matthew Granovetter
320pp., PB   Can $19.95   US $14.95

Partnership Bidding *a workbook* by Mary Paul
96pp., PB   Can $9.95   US $7.95

Playing with the Bridge Legends by Barnet Shenkin
(forewords by Zia and Michael Rosenberg)
240pp., PB   Can $24.95   US $17.95

The Pocket Guide to Bridge by Barbara Seagram and Ray Lee
64pp., PB   Can $9.95   US $7.95

Richelieu Plays Bridge by Robert F. MacKinnon
220pp., PB   Can $24.95   US $17.95

Saints and Sinners *The St. Titus Bridge Challenge* by David Bird & Tim Bourke
192pp., PB   Can $19.95   US $14.95

Samurai Bridge *A tale of old Japan* by Robert F. MacKinnon
256pp., PB   Can $ 22.95   US $16.95

Tales out of School *'Bridge 101' and other stories* by David Silver
(foreword by Dorothy Hayden Truscott)
128pp., PB   Can $ 12.95   US $9.95

The Bridge Magicians by Mark Horton and Radoslaw Kielbasinski
248pp., PB   Can $24.95   US $17.95

The Bridge Player's Bedside Book edited by Tony Forrester
256pp., HC   Can $27.95   US $19.95

The Bridge World's 'Test Your Play' by Jeff Rubens
164pp., PB   Can.$14.95   US $11.95

The Complete Book of BOLS Bridge Tips edited by Sally Brock
176pp., PB (photographs)   Can $24.95   US$17.95

There Must Be A Way... *52 challenging bridge hands* by Andrew Diosy
(foreword by Eddie Kantar)
96pp., PB   Can $9.95   US $9.95

Thinking on Defense *The art of visualization at bridge* by Jim Priebe
197pp., PB   Can $ 19.95   US $15.95

To Bid or Not to Bid by Larry Cohen
197pp., PB   Can $ 19.95   US $15.95

You Have to See This... *52 more challenging bridge problems*
by Andrew Diosy and Linda Lee
96pp., PB   Can $12.95   US $9.95

Win the Bermuda Bowl with Me by Jeff Meckstsroth and Marc Smith
188pp., PB   Can $24.95   US $17.95

World Class — conversations with the bridge masters
by Marc Smith
288pp., PB (photographs)   Can $24.95   US $17.95